PEOPLE NEED TO KNOW

Studies in the Postmodern Theory of Education

Shirley R. Steinberg
General Editor

Vol. 484

The Counterpoints series is part of the Peter Lang Education list.
Every volume is peer reviewed and meets
the highest quality standards for content and production.

PETER LANG
New York • Bern • Frankfurt • Berlin
Brussels • Vienna • Oxford • Warsaw

ROBERT M. LUCAS

PEOPLE NEED TO KNOW

CONFRONTING HISTORY IN THE HEARTLAND

PETER LANG
New York • Bern • Frankfurt • Berlin
Brussels • Vienna • Oxford • Warsaw

Library of Congress Cataloging-in-Publication Data

Names: Lucas, Robert M., author.
Title: People need to know: confronting history in the heartland /
Robert M. Lucas.
Description: New York: Peter Lang, [2016] | Series: Counterpoints:
studies in the postmodern theory of education, ISSN 1058-1634; vol. 484 |
Includes bibliographical references and index.
Identifiers: LCCN 2015033939 | ISBN 9781433129797 (hardcover: alk. paper) |
ISBN 9781433129780 (paperback: alk. paper) | ISBN 9781453915363 (e-book)
Subjects: LCSH: Local history—Study and teaching—Indiana—Marion. |
Outreach programs in history—Indiana—Marion. |
Lynching—Indiana—Marion—History—20th century. |
Marion (Indiana)—History—20th century.
Classification: LCC F534.M34 L84 2016 | DDC 977.2/69—dc23
LC record available at http://lccn.loc.gov/2015033939

Bibliographic information published by **Die Deutsche Nationalbibliothek**.
Die Deutsche Nationalbibliothek lists this publication in the "Deutsche
Nationalbibliografie"; detailed bibliographic data are available
on the Internet at http://dnb.d-nb.de/.

Cover art courtesy of the Indiana Historical Society, (PO411)
Changes made to the original item include cropping, superimposition, and tinting.

The paper in this book meets the guidelines for permanence and durability
of the Committee on Production Guidelines for Book Longevity
of the Council of Library Resources.

29 Broadway, 18th floor, New York, NY 10006
www.peterlang.com

Printed in the United States of America

CONTENTS

ACKNOWLEDGMENTS

My debts to Bill Munn are woven throughout the pages of this book, as, I hope, is my gratitude. As my teacher in the 1990s, Bill treated students with a level of intellectual respect that I had never before experienced, confronting us with complex issues, asking us to grapple with readings from real historians, and sparking in me a sense of intellectual excitement that continues to this day. By turning his abundant curiosity and initiative to focus on local issues, he modeled an admirably critical and yet constructive brand of civic engagement. Many times during the course of the research, I have reflected on the strength of my own complicated attachment to Marion, which owes a great deal to Bill's teaching in high school and beyond. Without his work over the decades and his extensive cooperation in 2011, this book would have been inconceivable. Thanks are also due to many others in Marion. These include, of course, Munn's students, whose conscientious work I continue to admire, and the members of the public who generously agreed to be interviewed. At the Marion Public Library, Rhonda Stoffer, Betty Reynolds, Joan Thomas, and Steve Collins supported our work, patiently answering questions and providing access to much-needed resources. Thanks also to John Beineke and Cynthia Carr for consultation in the very early stages of the research and to those other staff members at the Marion Public Library and Marion Community Schools who have supported the Community History Project over the years.

At Stanford, I am deeply grateful to John Willinsky, my doctoral adviser and dissertation chair, who provided guidance at every stage of this research. Through the ups and downs of a long and complex project, John has been unfailingly supportive, generous with his time, and flexible in helping me craft an argument that is true to my interests and values. Thanks also to my committee members Sam Wineburg, Shelley Goldman, and Ray McDermott for their support and feedback throughout the research process. Besides teaching me a great deal about history education, it was Sam who initially encouraged me to expand a term paper on the lynching and its memory into a larger research effort. Shelley provided wise counsel on issues of educational technology and qualitative research. Ray stoked my interest in pragmatism and shared a few well-placed, trenchant insights that caused me to rethink important issues. My university chair, Paula Findlen, also made helpful comments on the finished dissertation. Of course, any shortcomings in the work are mine alone.

This research was supported by Stanford's Dissertation Support Grant, which I thank for covering the costs of materials, travel, and other expenses associated with the research. A New Faculty Start-Up Grant from East Carolina University has supported follow-up research as well as some costs associated with the transition from dissertation to book. The Community History Project received early support from the Kellogg Foundation, without which none of the work described here would have been possible. Thanks to Shirley Steinberg, Chris Myers, and Bernadette Shade at Peter Lang for seeing this book through to publication.

I have been blessed by a wonderful group of friends and colleagues who have always been ready to provide support and advice. While conducting this research, the line between the personal and intellectual has always been highly permeable, and many of the same people have both commented on proposals and drafts and provided personal support and advice. Among many others, I would particularly like to thank Melissa Towne, Ethan Hutt, Julie Cohen, Matt Kloser, Tenelle Porter, Lara Buchak, Rachel Baker, Kenji Hakuta, and members of the Stanford History Education Group. Finally, thanks to my family—to my sisters, Sarah and Joanna, and to my parents, Robert and Patricia, who worked hard to instill and demonstrate the values reflected in this work: the love of learning, the importance of history, and the call of service. Their examples have surely shaped me in the most enduring ways possible.

INTRODUCTION

> What ever happened to the passion we all had to improve ourselves, live up to our potential, leave a mark on the world? Our hottest arguments were always about how we could *contribute*.
>
> —Wallace Stegner, *Crossing to Safety* (1987, p. 11, emphasis in original)

Late one morning in May 2011, I walked through the doorway of a newly opened, locally owned coffeehouse in Marion, Indiana, my hometown. The owner and I had never met—I left Marion for college in 1999 and lived in California—but she immediately recognized me as my father's son. At the counter, chatting with the owner and another middle-aged woman standing behind the register, I explained why I had returned that spring.

I was visiting from Stanford University, where I was studying education as a doctoral student, and I had come back to conduct research at Marion High School, my alma mater, in the classroom of my own former U.S. history teacher, Bill Munn. Since the mid-1990s, when I was a student, Mr. Munn and his classes had undertaken a series of experiments in local public history, conducting research on their—our—community's past. The students' projects, in addition to being graded and returned to them, were put to various uses: shown to younger students, archived at the local public library, sometimes even included in a printed book or published on the Internet. As Munn pithily remarked to me one day between periods in 2011, over the din of students moving from one class to the next, "people are so wedded to the disposable project.... This, to me, is bizarre." He explained, "If a kid goes to all the trouble—I don't want to see that end up in a wastebasket.... I mean, a kid might save it, but the utility of the project is completely gone. Who's the audience?" This is, in fragment, the idea I had returned to investigate. I hoped to find out what would happen if, to borrow a word from the novelist and historian Wallace Stegner, we let students learn while doing work that *contributes* to the world outside the school—and while arguing about how best to do so. What are the implications of this kind of project for students' motivation, for their understanding of history and the world they had inherited, and for the larger public at which their work was aimed?

I attempted to explain this to the two women, but at the mention of Mr. Munn's name, I recorded in my notes, the cashier's "face... brighten[ed] into a smile." Her son had been Munn's student and had completed a local history project, and she admired Munn's work. He was, she said, "an activist for very good causes." We spoke for a few more minutes—filling in the details for the owner, discussing her renovations to the shop—and then I took a seat to flesh out a set of field notes I had taken during a class earlier that morning.

I made a habit of returning to the shop between classes—there or the public library—to finish the morning's work and to ready myself for a second class in the afternoon. This coffeehouse, called the Spencer House, was a house in the literal sense: a 1920s Craftsman, painted apple green. From my usual seat at the front window, I looked out on the intersection of Spencer Avenue and the four-lane road known to area residents simply as "the bypass." Today, the bypass—officially, Martin Luther King, Jr. Memorial Way—is the city's main thoroughfare, a faceless strip of fast-food restaurants and neon signs, anchored at one end by a 1970s-era shopping mall, well past its prime, and at the other by a flourishing Walmart. Spencer Avenue, by contrast, is the location of some of Marion's most prestigious historic homes, and it leads off to the east, toward the stately Grant County Courthouse and its surrounding public square. Under different circumstances, Marion's square might be lively or even quaint, but here, today, as in many midwestern downtowns, most of the storefronts are empty, and businesses have long since migrated to the road once built to divert traffic around it. Unlike most other town squares, Marion's downtown also holds a more somber significance, the product of a gruesome episode of racial violence, decades old. This stain on the city's public life, and the efforts of a group of students to make sense of and address it, are at the center of this book, as I will shortly explain.

Marion is a small industrial city located seventy miles north of Indianapolis, near an interstate highway that leads to Fort Wayne and on to the auto factories of Michigan. Originally settled in the 1820s and 1830s, Marion's population later surged with the discovery of natural gas fields, increasing from about 3,000 in 1880 to more than 17,000 at the turn of the century (U.S. Census Bureau, 1880, 1900). The gas deposits were soon exhausted, but the town continued to grow. In all of this, Marion resembles its "gas boom" neighbor to the southeast, Muncie, which is best known as "Middletown" in Robert and Helen Lynd's classic study of class in a representative U.S. city (1929). Marion, too, is mostly "an ordinary place," says the Indiana University historian James Madison, by way of introduction to his study of the city and its sadly extraordinary racial history (2001, p. 3). It prospered as a factory town, first making glass as part of an industrial ecosystem that, in Muncie, produced the more famous Ball jars, and later making electronics for RCA and auto parts for General Motors. Recent decades have been less kind. With a succession of factory closings, Marion's population has declined from a peak near 40,000 in 1970 to just fewer than 30,000 in the 2010 census (U.S. Census Bureau, 1970, 2010).

Taking Indianapolis or even Muncie as a point of comparison, Marion is decidedly less cosmopolitan, with about half the population of the latter city. In place of Muncie's Ball State University, Marion is home to Indiana Wesleyan University, a once-moribund religious college that has grown sharply through the 1990s and 2000s. As this might suggest, Marion is a religious town. Until 1987, it was home to the headquarters of the Wesleyan Church, an evangelical Christian denomination, and although the offices have moved to the northern suburbs of Indianapolis, the town is still dotted with Wesleyan churches and organizations (Booher, 2004). As one student, the daughter of a Wesleyan pastor, told me in an interview, "every other street you get on, there's a Wesleyan church." At the beginning of my research that spring, I asked students to describe the city as they knew it. Among their most frequent responses (rivaled only by "boring" and the like), the students reminded me that Marion is a sports-loving town—specifically, a basketball town. It is a particular point of local pride that in the history of Indiana's famously intense high school basketball tournament, an annual event immortalized in the movie *Hoosiers*, Marion High School's team has won seven championships, trailing only Muncie Central's eight.

Most residents would prefer that the town be associated with athletic greatness, but I returned that spring to work with students in researching another matter, arguably the most significant event in Marion's history. Many of its details are murky, but to make comprehensible the investigations described in the chapters to come, I trace its basic arc here. I rely primarily on James Madison's authoritative 2001 history, supplemented by a later book from journalist and critic Cynthia Carr (2006). About the precipitating events, one thing is certain: On the evening of August 6, 1930, a white twenty-four-year-old man named Claude Deeter was shot. He had parked on a Lovers' Lane on the edge of town with a white eighteen-year-old woman, Mary Ball, who was referenced in newspaper accounts of the event as his fiancée. Three young African American men—Tommy Shipp, nineteen; Abram Smith, eighteen; and James Cameron, sixteen—approached the car in what seems to have been an attempted robbery. In Cameron's later account of the events, he fled, having recognized Deeter as his shoeshine customer and, he said, a friend. Over his shoulder, Cameron heard the shot that inflicted the wound of which Deeter would later die (Cameron, 1982/1994). This version of the shooting is impossible to verify, but it is not usually challenged.

According to newspaper reports at the time, Ball alleged rape—and this, not the shooting, seems to have spurred the formation of an angry mob the following day—but when questioned at the hospital, the fatally wounded Deeter made no mention of a rape, and doubt was later cast on Ball's claim (Madison, 2001, pp. 5, 67–69). There were rumors, in the years after, that Mary Ball and the three accused boys had formed a stickup gang, with Ball luring in unsuspecting victims. Others claimed that Ball was a prostitute, or at the center of a love triangle with Deeter and Smith, or that the five were all criminals fighting over money. At the very least, it seems clear that Deeter and Ball were not engaged, as newspapers initially reported (Carr, 2006, pp. 35–36; Madison, 2001, pp. 67–69, 102, 107).

Shipp, Smith, and Cameron were arrested in their homes late on the night of the shooting, and Deeter died the following afternoon at Marion General Hospital. The evening of that second day, August 7, a mob assembled in Marion, took sledgehammers from a nearby factory, and advanced on the Grant County Jail where the men were being held. Local authorities, led by Sheriff Jake Campbell, resisted for about thirty minutes before surrendering control. At approximately 10:30 p.m., Shipp was pulled from the jail and hanged to his death, outside, on the bars of a prison window. His body was taken to the courthouse square a block away, hoisted from a tree branch, and mutilated. The second boy, Abram Smith, was beaten outside the jail and dragged the block to the square. He was still living when lynched from the tree. Finally, James Cameron was pulled from the jail and taken to the courthouse lawn (Madison, 2001, pp. 9–10). Decades later, Cameron told of the subsequent events as follows:

> With the noose around my neck and death in my brain, I waited for the end. But before the crowd could hang me, a voice rose above the deafening roar of the mob. It was an echo-like voice that seemed to come from some far-away place. It was a feminine voice, sweet, clear, but unlike anything I had ever heard. It was sharp and crisp, like bells ringing out on a clear, cold winter day.
>
> *"Take this boy back. He had nothing to do with any raping or killing!"*
>
> That was all the voice said.
>
> Abruptly, impossibly, silence fell over that raging mob, as if they had been struck dumb. No one moved or spoke a word.... Time stood still for that one instant. The fury of that mob had been quelled in the moment. (Cameron, 1982/1994, pp. 73–75, emphasis in original)

According to Madison, the voice was reported independently by multiple sources, but the identity of the speaker has never been established (2001, p. 10). Cameron was convinced that it was the voice of an angel. The mob's fury subsided, but men and women, perpetrators and other residents, continued to mill about the square. Lawrence Beitler, a local photographer, moved his tripod, flash powder, and eight-by-ten-inch view camera from his studio two blocks to the square and took a picture of the suspended corpses and the crowd of smiling spectators beneath. He would sell prints, in the following days, for fifty cents apiece (Madison, 2001, pp. 6–11).

Questions remain about many details of the event. Who led the mob, and who is captured in the photograph? Two men were tried and acquitted. Mary's father, Hoot Ball, was a confirmed leader but was never charged. Other names were said to be widely known; journalist Cynthia Carr has collected some but has not divulged them (Carr, 2006; Madison, 2001, p. 67). In legal depositions, nearly all witnesses claimed the mob was composed of strangers from out of town, but these have the ring of evasions from a fearful or sympathetic populace (Madison, 2001, pp. 81–85). Some say that plans for the lynching were afoot even before Deeter's death. Marion's beloved "boy mayor," Jack Edwards, a friend to the black community who remains to this day the premiere politician in town history, left Marion for Indianapolis the afternoon of the lynching. Had he been warned (Carr, 2006, p. 36)? How large was the mob, and where did the members come from (Madison, 2001, pp. 83–84)? How much of a fight was put up by law enforcement? Madison emphasizes their resistance and their use of tear gas (Madison, 2001, pp. 8, 85). Carr repeats stories about Sheriff Campbell throwing the keys to the jail to the mob. She was also told by Cameron and a ninety-four-year-old Jack Edwards that Campbell was a Klan member, at least before the Indiana Klan collapsed in the mid-1920s (Carr, 2006, pp. 24, 34–35, 65–66). Above all, whose voice calmed the mob, and why was Cameron allowed to live?

Marion's black residents huddled in their homes fearing further attacks, while local NAACP leader Flossie Bailey called state officials and the national NAACP, seeking protection and investigation. The violence was over by 11 p.m., though a crowd lingered well past midnight. Marion's police cut down the corpses early the following morning, and detectives began a half-hearted inquiry, but they found few people willing to talk. NAACP acting director Walter White, who had been the organization's investigator of such crimes, visited the town at Bailey's behest and compiled a list of suspected mob members, which he provided to the authorities. Bailey, whose role Madison stresses in pursuing justice for the two men murdered by the mob, went on to push for and win the passage of a state anti-lynching law, under which any sheriff who allowed the lynching of a prisoner would be immediately removed from his position and could be sued for damages (Madison, 2001, pp. 10–11, 63–67, 89–96).

Lawrence Beitler's photograph (see Figure 1) ran widely in newspapers in the days after the event and has, over the years, become one of America's most recognizable images of racism's scourge in twentieth-century America. To this day, however, it has not appeared in Marion's daily newspaper, the *Chronicle-Tribune*. Its appearance in a New York newspaper is thought to have inspired a high school teacher in the Bronx, Abel Meeropol, to pen the anti-lynching poem "Strange Fruit," which he published in a union magazine and later set to music. Interpreted by Billie Holiday, the resulting song became a landmark of social protest and was later named the Song of the Century by *Time* magazine (Margolick, 2001).[1]

Figure 1: Photograph taken by Lawrence Beitler in Marion on the night of August 7, 1930. (Courtesy Indiana Historical Society PO411)

Cameron was convicted as an accessory to voluntary manslaughter in the death of Claude Deeter eleven months after the lynching. Prosecutors dropped charges of rape, murder, auto banditry, and robbery. Cameron was sentenced to serve two to ten years in the state reformatory—lenient in consideration of Cameron's youth, it was said (Madison, 2001, pp. 107–108). He was paroled after four years and moved between several Indiana cities before settling in 1953 in Milwaukee, Wisconsin. In 1978, in retirement, Cameron and his wife visited the museum at Israel's Yad Vashem Holocaust Memorial, and he set upon the idea of creating a similar museum about American lynching. Over the next decade, he used personal funds to create the America's Black Holocaust Museum in Milwaukee. Meanwhile, Cameron wrote and self-published a first-person account of the lynching, *A Time of Terror*, which was later republished by Black Classic Press (1982/1994). The book was excerpted in *Ebony* magazine and earned Cameron coverage from numerous national news outlets, including the *Oprah Winfrey Show*, the *CBS Evening News*, and other venues of similar prominence (Madison, 2001, pp. 119, 120, 126).

Events of the 1990s and 2000s have brought some limited measure of healing. In 1993, at a tearful ceremony in downtown Marion, Cameron was granted an official pardon by then-governor Evan Bayh and was presented with a key to the city. In November 1998, an African American son of Marion—a high-school track star and successful FBI agent—returned home and was elected sheriff. Widely interpreted as a moment of redemption, the election prompted headlines such as "Town With Tainted Past Elects First Black Sheriff in Indiana" (1998). Three documentaries about the lynching have been filmed (Garrett, 1994; Gould, 1998; Sapin, 1995), one by the BBC and two by PBS affiliates, and two additional books have been published. James Madison's history of the event, already noted, appeared in 2001. Cynthia Carr, who had spent childhood summers in Marion visiting grandparents, wrote an article about Cameron's pardon for the *Village Voice*, which she then expanded into the book *Our Town*, a work partly of memoir, partly of journalistic investigation (2006).

In 2003, a peak year in recent activity, a "Day of Forgiveness" was organized by twenty local ministers, ten black and ten white. As originally proposed, the event would have culminated in the unveiling of a reconciliation monument on the courthouse lawn. But when this plan was announced, the response was swift and negative. As the event's lead African American organizer, Rev. Larry Batchelor, told Carr, "I got calls from white folk and black folk wailing, 'Leave it alone. It'll go away'" (Carr, 2006, p. 465). The monument was reduced to an obliquely worded plaque, to be posted inside the courthouse rather than outside where the tree had stood. Eventually, the plans for a physical memorial were abandoned entirely, although a church service went forward and was, by Carr's account, quite moving. There is to this day no permanent marker. In 2005, Cameron was in attendance when the U.S. Senate issued an official apology for having failed to pass a federal anti-lynching law. Cameron died the following year, aged ninety-two ("James Cameron, 92, Founder of Museum, Is Dead," 2006).

I returned to Marion in 2011 to study and participate in an effort to remember the lynching, not with a physical memorial but with a series of web pages. This work was undertaken as part of the Community History Project (CHP), a program founded in the mid-1990s by history teacher Bill Munn as a partnership between Marion High School and the Marion Public Library. Mr. Munn was my teacher then, and mine was one of the first classes to participate in the CHP. In the fifteen years since, Munn and the students had experimented with many different kinds of projects, including papers, oral histories, documentary videos, and interactive media, covering everything from town heroes to historic buildings. Student papers in the CHP were most often filed at the public library with some of the best collected in a printed volume or posted on the web.

The CHP did not change my life, at least not right away, but I saw it become important to two close friends, who spent countless hours producing a series of documentary videos that were screened at the public library, in local middle and elementary schools, and at meetings around the state (Sickler, 1998; Voss, 1998; Voss & Sickler, 1999). My own project was less transformative: I interviewed a city councilman about his role in founding the Marion Easter Pageant and helped, on the side, with some microfilm work. I certainly remember the experiences and found some of the material compelling, but, as I recall, I was most interested in issues of national and international scope—and in my scores on the Advanced Placement U.S. History test, which I hoped would help me leave the small-town Midwest behind.

Munn and I remained in touch as I went off to college, became a social studies teacher myself, and then pursued a master's degree in educational technology. In 2007, I found myself spending a few months home in Marion, before beginning a doctoral program in education at Stanford, and during that time I worked with Munn to create the framework of a new website, WikiMarion.org. Though we have never allowed open editing in the way a site like Wikipedia does, this format allowed the publication of more work by people with less technical facility than had the previous CHP website. We posted old student projects there, assisted by a retired English teacher and former collaborator. I also taught students to use the site, and some have posted new work in the years since.

I remained involved during my subsequent years of graduate study, albeit more peripherally, and so the CHP remained close to my thoughts as I read educational theory and reassessed the state of schools and school reforms. For reasons suggested above and further elaborated in Chapter 2, I became interested in the way the CHP, unlike so many videos, worksheets, tests, and papers, channeled students' effort toward a valuable product, offering them the opportunity to learn while doing something worthwhile in the world. Far from a relic of my childhood, the project spoke to concerns about the current educational moment. To be specific: standardized testing, in order to ensure comparable measurement across contexts, calls for environments that are uniform and sealed off from outside influences. As the educational system becomes increasingly structured around this form of assessment, I fear that learning environments—isolated from the surrounding community even to begin with—will come to reflect these assumptions more completely than they already do. These, of course, run counter to the assumptions and educational values embedded in the CHP. They constrain opportunities for students to interact with, and draw motivation from, the world outside the learning and assessment context. Moreover, by imposing identical standards everywhere, they limit the attention that can be paid to local contexts or to students' pursuit of personal interests that could otherwise be guided into worthy academic inquiries. Even in Munn's classroom, in 2011, I saw the pressures toward content coverage threaten to crowd out his and his students' more innovative work. Curricular and pedagogical issues, then, are at the center of this book. The text delves deep into the context of one community and the details of one historical event. The details of that case are gravely important, and by showing how students made sense of and acted upon them, I hope to draw a portrait of learning that is public, historically contextualized, socially engaged, and ethically responsible.

Although the pedagogical approach portrayed in this book runs counter to the general thrust of standardizing educational reforms, it is entirely in step with other cultural trends, especially as regards the social and technological changes under way in an Internet era that has now reached early middle age. Recent decades have seen a steady proliferation of tools and practices that enable people to more easily develop, produce, and share ideas and culture (Benkler, 2006, Ch. 6). An ever-lengthening list would include Wikipedia, blogging, free and open source software, academic databases, the Project Gutenberg book repository, Open Access publishing, podcasting, photo and video sharing, e-book publishing, and the so-called maker movement of material design and creation (for the last, see Blikstein, 2014). These developments do more than lend legitimacy and currency to a production-oriented curricular program: They suggest the multiple avenues through which student work can reach a public audience; they provide source material on which students can draw; and they create a context of audiences, conversations, and histories in which meaningful work can take place. Certain widely used educational practices can be helpful in addressing these trends—there are resonances with performance assessment and project-based learning, as discussed in Chapter 2—but even these are insufficiently attentive to the *contribution* made by student work and its *value* in the public culture. It is my hope that this book will provide a better sense of the ways in which students' projects can realize values, for themselves and others, and can help to refine technologies and practices that facilitate further such work.

The CHP also points to a way of assessing student learning that stands as an alternative to tests and the technological universe that has grown up around them. It suggests that for engaged citizens, oversight need not be carried out by monitoring the ups and downs of the local schools' composite test scores, but by examining student work aimed at creating value and then by judging whether, to what extent, and in what ways it succeeds. Such a process, it seems to me, points toward a deeper sort of public involvement in the assessment process and invites a more nuanced conversation about the goals and contributions of public education. It should be said that although "high-stakes testing" is a common bugbear of progressive educational reform, the approach explored here does not represent a lowering of stakes. To the contrary, as Madison observes in an interview I will discuss in Chapter 5, public work raises the stakes, not by placing ever-heavier consequences on a few hours of testing but by increasing the real-world import and value of students' day-to-day work.

For all of these reasons I came to think, over the course of my graduate education, that the CHP was worthy of systematic study. By 2011, however, time was running short. Munn began to speak of retirement, and while we hoped the work would continue on in some form, it seemed advantageous to examine it in his classroom where it had developed, the better to learn from the project's accumulated wisdom. Munn's looming transition also marked a last chance of sorts for treatment of the lynching. He had taught students about the event every year, and their CHP projects had addressed it occasionally—videos were produced on James Cameron and Flossie Bailey and articles were written about the courthouse and jail—but many topics remained unexplored. Munn and I had long agreed that something more comprehensive was needed, but the project had not been carried out, perhaps because of its perceived sensitivity and complexity or because it was being researched in such great depth by others like Madison and Carr, while other topics susceptible to student research went neglected. With all of these concerns in mind, I returned in spring 2011—Bill Munn's forty-second and final year of teaching—to study this approach to learning, while also pushing it to a place Munn had not been able to go alone, working with a group of students as they researched the lynching and created a set of pages about it for WikiMarion.org.

A few remarks are in order about why I chose to study a project on a topic as singular as the Marion lynching, which complicates questions of generalization to other classrooms. First, it presented a real opportunity to do something worthwhile—a prerequisite for value-oriented work. If this borders on tautology, my point is simply that any project of this sort entails finding some combination of important topics, available sources, unmet needs, and powerful stories. Munn and I found these in the lynching, and other teachers would do well to seek out similarly urgent topics in their own communities. Still, this topic and this photograph are unusually striking, more so than many other worthy topics a class might undertake, so let me be clear: Although the CHP arose in a setting that is in many ways ordinary, the research at hand offers an extreme case rather than a typical one. The lynching is complex and sensitive, potentially controversial yet also in constant danger of being papered over. Thus, it promised to cast in sharp relief the range of opportunities and challenges that are possible in public work.

A second issue also distinguishes this project from others that Munn or another teacher might undertake—namely, my presence. As a participant-observer, I spent time documenting the work, but I also participated actively and extensively, as characterized in Chapter 3. It became clear over the course of the work that although the students' individual projects were comparable in scope to others conducted through the years, the variety among them would have made the effort as a whole too complicated for one teacher to oversee alone, at least in the relatively paltry class time allotted—roughly ten to twelve hours spaced over eight weeks.[2] By participating in this way, I was able to better gain the students' trust and to learn about a wider range of projects than would otherwise have been possible. My role also allowed me to experience the project, in some ways, from a teacher's perspective and to discuss it with Munn accordingly. I came to better appreciate, for example, the need for tolerance of projects that develop in different ways and at different rates, with the inevitable scheduling and technical difficulties, and to better understand how the project places the teacher in a new relationship to community members. At the same time, along with these advantages, the presence of a second, knowledgeable adult made the setting less like a typical high school class.

My role and the relationships I developed also added to my personal stake in this work. As should by now be apparent, I was invested in the project in a variety of ways. Marion is important to me, and I hoped the project would do justice to the lynching and contribute positively to the community. While conducting research as a participant-observer, I worked toward that goal, just as I suggest students and teachers might do. My familiarity with Marion enhances my ability to contextualize the project, and my ties in the community gave me access to the CHP itself and to interviewees. But, by the same token, this means I have relationships to preserve—with Munn, with the students, and with the town as a whole. Finally, I have an ethical interest in the questions being asked. I posed them because I thought they were important and that they could help contribute to meaningful learning experiences and a vibrant public sphere.

In light of my deep investment in the CHP and this research, I can make no pretense of being entirely an objective observer. Work of *value* is work that impinges upon one's *values*. By emphasizing this aspect of scholarship, for the students and myself, I signal my conviction that it is better to take on matters of personal and social importance than to search for some point, outside of one's social and historical position, from which objective observation is possible. My approach, then, is to disclose the sources of my investment and to attempt an even-handed analysis.[3] To accomplish this, I sought out evidence that would contradict my assumptions and show the limits of this sort of learning—which is to say, its relative weaknesses compared with other sorts of learning activities, limits to the depth of learning and the quality of work that can be expected of still-developing adolescents, and opportunities for learning that Munn and I did not seize, but which teachers could be helped to recognize and exploit.

This book describes a set of highly compelling learning experiences, but I do not claim that all worthwhile projects need be organized around the idea of public value. This much may be obvious, but as I have said, my own CHP project was basically unremarkable, in terms of its effects on both me and others. Curiously, it was a more traditional piece of writing, completed for that same class, that most immediately altered the course of my life. My interests at the time ran to the national and global, and Mr. Munn, sensitive to this, alerted me to an essay contest sponsored by the U.S. Institute of Peace (USIP), which I entered as an alternative assignment. My essay, which examined post-war justice and truth and reconciliation commissions in Japan and El Salvador, was never intended to see a public audience (aside from contest judges), and I had no expectation that my analysis would make any new contribution, and yet I threw myself into the work, printing articles from the public library's electronic databases and requesting scholarly books through interlibrary loan. My essay won the state-level first prize.

The USIP convened a weeklong conference of state winners in Washington, DC, where we visited landmarks, were briefed at embassies, and took part in simulated negotiations. The week culminated in a final awards banquet, with assigned seating, but as I searched in vain for my place card, a staffer told me of a last-minute change—a vice president of the institute had requested that I be switched to his table. The dinner passed uneventfully and without further explanation, but as the event came to a close and people stood to leave, the vice president, a Mr. Chick Nelson, caught my attention. Here, I can only paraphrase as I remember, with the inevitable distortions of time and repeated retelling: "Rob," he said, "you may have wondered why I asked to have you at this table. I graduated from Marion High School in 1948. Every year, I look for the Indiana winner of this contest, and never has one come from Marion, until now." Nelson had gone from Marion to Harvard, well beyond the horizons of most small-town students, and had helped several younger schoolmates to follow in the years immediately after. Later in the summer of 1998, he returned to Marion for his fiftieth high school reunion. We met again, began to develop a relationship, and he eventually encouraged me to apply to Harvard, submitting a letter of recommendation on my behalf. I was accepted and chose to attend. At Harvard, I joined a program teaching international issues to Boston-area high school students, also writing curriculum and bringing students to campus each semester for a simulated global summit. After graduating, I became a social studies teacher myself. Sixteen years later, and, as Robert Frost says, "knowing how way leads on to way," I can hardly conceive of my life as it might have unfolded without that class project.

My experience with the USIP essay competition bears certain hallmarks of Munn's teaching style: flexibility, attention to student interest, and an inclination to reach outside the school to invest projects with larger significance. Nevertheless, this was one of the most significant educational events of my life despite the fact that it lacked the defining feature explored in this book: My paper itself never became public and would have had little impact if it did. As I argue for a certain kind of class project, then, it is with the understanding that there are important educational values that may be best achieved by other means.

In light of these cautions, what sort of conclusions can be drawn? I argue first that when considering the shortcomings of existing classrooms and curricula, we should pay attention to the value of the work students are asked to produce. I present, on the order of an existence proof, an example of an activity intended to create public value and, then, an analysis of the varied kinds of value that students and members of the public perceived in it. These values include, but are not limited to, knowledge and skill development, an evolving sense of history and the status of historical knowledge, and a developing personal relationship to Marion and its painful past. They include, likewise, the value to the community of the products they made—in artifacts created, perspectives captured, information synthesized, and access increased, among many others. Finally, by participating in history making in this public context, I hope to show that students can develop a sort of historical understanding that goes beyond those that are traditionally recognized—one that, because it unfolds in the context of valuable public work, is imbued with particularly compelling intellectual, social, and emotional meanings.

The lynching project can, I think, fairly be called a success. I regard it as one, and based on the evidence put forward in the chapters to come, I expect that many readers will agree. It was appreciated by members of the public (including historians who were familiar with the event), provided a positive experience for most or all participating students and affected some in profound ways. However, owing to the nature of the research and the open-endedness of the pedagogical strategy, I do not claim to give ironclad evidence that the approach *works* in any simple or definitive way, or that it would necessarily achieve similar results if implemented in other contexts. Indeed, the implications of this research will undoubtedly vary across sites, school subjects, and grade levels, and the potential results of this sort of project depend substantially on decisions made by teachers and students in each individual case. My aim is to show what powerful sorts of learning can take place when the public value of students' work projects is considered as an important outcome of educational activities and, thus, to show why such learning merits a place in the curriculum.

The book is laid out as follows: In conducting this research, I am also testing the founding assumptions of the CHP, and so I show in Chapter 1 that the CHP was animated by ideas about community, history, and learning, not least among them the supposition that students can learn while making worthwhile public contributions. This chapter also serves to contextualize the work I studied in 2011, shedding light on the development of the CHP, the variety of student projects that have been undertaken, the learning that Munn has derived from this activity, and the ways in which, through this work, he has taken on the role of a local public intellectual. In Chapter 2, I discuss the theoretical sources of the questions I brought to this work, situating them and the project within a tradition of product- and project-oriented curricular programs beginning with Dewey. In Chapter 3, I explain how the lynching project itself was carried out, showing the process undertaken, further clarifying my role and attempting to capture something of the knowledge and practice that make this work possible. Chapter 4 focuses on students' perspectives, presenting their reflections on the value of the work based on interviews conducted at project's end. In evaluating a project aimed at creating value beyond the school, it is necessary to speak with members of the prospective audience, so in Chapter 5 I report on interviews with a variety of community members including historians and those from other walks of life. These community members were asked to examine student work and assess the project's quality and value, and, by and large, they gave it a positive evaluation. Finally, in the conclusion, I consider the work's broader implications—for teaching and learning in other contexts, for the development of educational technologies, and for learning theory more generally. In the course of these chapters it is occasionally necessary to explain how evidence was obtained, but in general, extended discussions of research design are confined to Appendix A.

In June 2011, a month after my first visit to the Spencer House coffeehouse, I returned again, this time bringing Munn along. The school year was over, the project complete, and we met there to debrief. Munn had just returned from a graders' conference for the Advanced Placement (AP) U.S. History test. This was his first such experience, and so our conversation also dealt with what he had learned there. With colleagues from across the country, he had been taught to score responses from the AP test's essay sections. He had also taken away lessons about how teachers can substantively improve their writing instruction and how students, by knowing how the test is scored, can eke out an extra point or two. He later emailed me the main points: "Have a strong thesis"; "Analyze the documents—don't simply mention them"; "Bring in outside information"; "Write legibly"; and finally, "Graders are not the enemy." Munn told me that he had spoken out against the test's multiple choice section and found the free response essays somewhat superficial but more satisfactory. The document-based question, he said, in which students are given a question to answer using a set of primary sources and their own background knowledge, was best of all at showing their learning.

As Munn and I talked, the proprietor approached our coffeehouse table and introduced herself. Was Mr. Munn the county historian? Hadn't his students researched the histories of local buildings? She had a story to share. An elderly couple had recently stopped by on their morning walk, bringing old photographs of the coffeehouse. The woman had lived there as a child, with twelve brothers and sisters, until her father had been struck by lightning and the children divided among orphanages. She wanted to know whether a student would want to research this.

The focus of this book is on public historical work, not AP-style assessments, but their juxtaposition demonstrates the sort of concern that motivates my inquiry. I stress that there is educational value in both. It is disconcerting, however, to consider that under traditional assumptions, students might need to be convinced that the one or two people who will read their work are not, in fact, "the enemy." In the following pages, I investigate the implications of a different set of assumptions. When members of the community approach a teacher for historical research, this suggests a different kind of public role for the teacher and school than is customary. And when students learn by making valuable contributions, whether to web surfers or a coffeehouse clientele, they are given an all-too-rare educational opportunity: to do something important and to learn firsthand why history matters.

· 1 ·

"LIFE IS AN EXPERIMENT"

Bill Munn moved to Marion in 1969 and was quickly confronted by the town's troubled history. Cynthia Carr recounts the story in her book on the lynching and its repercussions: "As [Munn] began teaching seventh grade in North Marion, he asked his all-white class to tell him something about the town, and one student immediately announced: 'We hung the niggers.' Munn also recalled white people offering to show him the lynching picture, saying, 'I've got it in the trunk of my car'" (2006, p. 377). These startling exchanges were not the point of origin for Munn's social concern—his history of activism dates back much further—but they did mark his first encounter with the issues of local injustice that would preoccupy him for decades to come.

Certain dispositions toward teaching have been present in Munn's work since the beginning, including an affinity for self-directed student projects and an experimental attitude toward his own teaching and learning. One afternoon in 2011, midway through our research project, I arrived for class, and Munn directed me to a favorite quotation written on the classroom whiteboard: "Life is an experiment"—Emerson, by way of Oliver Wendell Holmes Jr. As Munn commented, that one brief line explained much of his work on the CHP. His experiments, I discovered, have yielded sustained learning, allowing Munn to refine community-based class projects, build knowledge of local narratives in which his students might become invested, and develop relationships that would help his classes conduct and disseminate their work. By the time of my visit, the fruits of Munn's experimentation were evident not only in his classroom practice but also in the role he had fashioned as a local public intellectual. Using media that changed over time, from newspaper columns and local radio segments to a blog and a preservationist Facebook group, Munn cultivated a public platform and persona that helped to magnify the value of his students' work and to embody, for his community, the possibility that a teacher might advance public learning both in and outside of the classroom.

Bill Munn

While hardly a traditionalist, Bill Munn sees himself and his work in continuity with the past, both with his lineal ancestors and the intellectual traditions to which he contributes.[1] His paternal grandfather, Jacob, was a teacher and school administrator—a progressive, he told me with evident pride, who studied at Teachers College in the 1920s, during Dewey's tenure and the heyday of William Heard Kilpatrick and the "project method." Jacob was also a devotee of the "social gospel" and a follower of the theologian Walter Rauschenbusch. His grandson, as a teacher and committed Episcopalian, carries both traditions forward.

Given Munn's associative style, our 2011 planning sessions often gave way to wide-ranging conversations that provided ample occasion to explore the roots and development of the CHP. In one such conversation, I asked about his commitment to experimentation, and he recalled the spirit of one of the formative documents of his youth, the Port Huron Statement. Munn was born and raised not in Marion but in the northeastern Indiana town of Angola, the son of a secretary and an administrator at Tri-State University (now Trine University) near the Indiana–Ohio–Michigan border. It was in Michigan, in 1962, that the Port Huron Statement was issued at the founding of Students for a Democratic Society. At this time, Munn was a high school student some two hundred miles to the south. He was affected profoundly by the statement, he told me, as he paraphrased from memory the document's ominous Cold War–era warning: "We may be the last generation in the experiment with living." The Port Huron Statement goes on to call for the creation of "a truly 'public sector'" brought about through "experiments in decentralization" that would give more people a voice in the political debates that affect their lives. In what is ostensibly an economic commentary but to me resembles nothing so much as a curricular manifesto, the authors declare "that work... should be educative, not stultifying; creative, not mechanical; self-directed, not manipulated, encouraging independence, a respect for others, a sense of dignity and a willingness to accept social responsibility" (Students for a Democratic Society, 1962). SDS took a more radical turn in the ensuing years, but this original document anticipates much of what Munn would later put to work in his teaching.

When Munn came to Marion in 1969, he had just finished undergraduate work at Ball State University, where he majored in U.S. history and political science. (He recalled meeting Robert Kennedy at a rally in Muncie in April 1968, just hours before Kennedy would inform an anguished Indianapolis audience of the death of Martin Luther King Jr.)[2] In his first years of teaching, Munn continued to take evening classes at Ball State, earning a master's degree in education in 1972. He taught middle school through most of the 1970s and coordinated a gifted-and-talented program in the 1980s, all the while leading two teachers' union strikes and, through his organizing efforts, learning much about Marion's social history. However formative these experiences may have been, though, the most important features of his community history work appeared only in the mid-1990s.

The Community History Project

Munn traces the beginnings of the CHP to a conversation that occurred in about 1995, when a student approached him with a special request. Her grandmother had grown up in a Mennonite orphanage, and she hoped to do a class project on this experience. Munn agreed, and the project was so successful, in its narrative quality and in the way it shed light on the experience of the Great Depression among marginalized groups, that he began considering how to incorporate more such work into his class. From there, the beginnings of the CHP are well documented in newspaper articles and grant applications. Munn told Marion's daily newspaper, the *Chronicle-Tribune*, that the idea was further developed in conversations with two English teachers with whom he co-taught an interdisciplinary sequence in American Studies: "We talked about how we really needed to pull these things down to a local level. If it's the Depression, World War I issues, how were those faced here? How were they faced by African Americans, the Miami [Indians], women?" (Smith, 1999).

Many of the projects I will describe emphasize local particularity, but this coexists, in the CHP, with a sense that local experiences can be seen as manifestations of larger-scale phenomena. This, if successful, relates the students' learning to state standards and history curricula even as it reaches closer to their daily lives. Besides instruction, the teachers' conversations touched on assessment as well: "We were trying to get away from the traditional semester test," Munn told the reporter. "To us, that was not a satisfactory way of judging what the students knew.... We were looking for alternatives for students to show their abilities" (Smith, 1999). This statement echoes concerns with "authentic" and "performance" assessments that are reflected, for example, in articles by Grant Wiggins that were then appearing in the sort of professional publications of which Munn was a reader (1989, 1993).

The first CHP assignment—a joint project carried out in history and English classes—was initiated in 1996–1997. Students each selected a year, beginning with 1885 and working forward. They then searched the microfilm of local newspapers for "three significant events in the history of Marion and Grant County from that year," about which they wrote term papers. Munn mentioned to the *Chronicle-Tribune* that issues of historical rigor were also kept in mind: "There was one rule. Everything found had to be documented by at least two sources" (Smith, 1999).[3] In that first project, Munn was delighted by the results:

> The kids came back with their research. It was just wonderful. Instead of just talking about the election of 1912, we found out that Theodore Roosevelt, Woodrow Wilson and William Howard Taft had come to Marion to make stump speeches. We found out how significant the WCTU [Women's Christian Temperance Union] was in Marion. Prior to women getting the right to vote there was an active and important women's movement in Marion. (Smith, 1997)

The students' work was also better than usual, Munn noticed, and "more original" (Smith, 1999). With the Port Huron Statement in mind, one can also see a veteran teacher injecting a bit of novelty and learning into potentially stultifying work. As Munn told the reporter in 1999, "How many papers can you read on the Gettysburg Address before your eyes glaze over? But when I read that eight weeks after the sinking of the *Titanic*, a group of steerage passengers who had survived stopped in Marion and were interviewed, that was something new" (Smith, 1999).

In 1997, on the strength of these early successes, Munn formed a partnership among the high school, the Marion Public Library, and the Community

Foundation of Grant County. He applied for and received a $40,000 grant from the Kellogg Foundation, which paid for computers and equipment, stipends, and travel expenses, and for reconstructing a documentary record by digitizing photographs and filling gaps in the reels of newspaper microfilm.[4] In the grant proposal, the stated goal of the project is to "engage cross generational populations in the creation, development, replication and dissemination of projects based on local history with special attention to populations and issues that would include the Miami Indians of Indiana (Eastern Band) and an African American community."[5] The major features of the CHP are all present in the proposal. The focus on race—African American issues most of all—carries through the life of the project. Students' participation is central, and the explicit goal is to make history relevant to their lives by grounding it in local matters. There in the proposal, too, is the idea that research is only as good as its means of publication; the text mentions that several students had already expressed interest in creating a website to distribute the work.

The overarching aim of the project, as its name suggests, was to build community by creating history. According to the proposal, the project would build "truly community history"—shades, again, of that other founding document, Port Huron—by working to "rescue and document disappearing histories" from diverse groups and then by using the Internet to make them widely accessible. By prompting people to work together, it was proposed, the project would allow "citizens... to collectively explore their life and build partnerships for the betterment of community understanding and life." That is, as people worked together to build history, the community would be strengthened by the shared self-understandings that they would develop and the social ties that would be established.

This argument is presented, in expanded form, in Robert Bellah and his colleagues' *Habits of the Heart* (1985), an analysis of community that Munn cites as an intellectual inspiration for his project. Community can be defined using a variety of criteria; Bellah and company emphasize shared practice and decision making while others mention joint goals, common beliefs, and other factors (Barab & Duffy, 2000). Most relevant here, however, is the role of history or memory, which is central to Bellah and colleagues' conception—so much so that they use "community" and "community of memory" essentially interchangeably (1985, p. 333). Bellah and colleagues' analysis of the role of history in forming communities provides a context for interpreting the CHP proposal and prefigures important areas of the project's work: "In order not to forget [its] past, a community is involved in retelling its story, its constitutive narrative, and in so doing, it offers examples of the men and women who have embodied and exemplified the meaning of the community" (1985, p. 153). This brings to mind "Marion Heroes," the title of a biographical project that Munn used several times through the years, and that now forms a section of the WikiMarion website. Because the student body is diverse, their topics tend to be as well. The CHP's focus on racial injustice, though, is better interpreted through another of Bellah and colleagues' observations: "A genuine community of memory will also tell painful stories of shared suffering that sometimes creates deeper identities than success.... And if the community is completely honest, it will remember stories not only of suffering received but of suffering inflicted—dangerous memories, for they call the community to alter ancient evils" (1985, p. 153). A CHP project like *Rough Times*, containing oral histories of the Great Depression and World War II, satisfies this first need (Munn, Bratton, & Lakes, 1999). The second—memory of suffering inflicted—is a less common research theme, but it factors in certain projects, like the work on segregation described below, and, of course, in research on the lynching. A project like Amy Coleman's 2007 documentary video on local NAACP head Flossie Bailey, which draws on Madison's research, bridges these categories by showing the heroism of an African American woman in the face of persecution. For Bellah and colleagues, the power of those memories comes not only in how they influence understandings but also in the way they compel social action—spur people to "alter" past wrongs and then make their own "contributions":

> The communities of memory that tie us to the past also turn us toward the future as communities of hope. They carry a context of meaning that can allow us to connect our aspirations for ourselves and those closest to us with the aspirations of a larger whole and see our own efforts as being, in part, contributions to a common good. (1985, p. 153)

By involving students in this kind of contribution, the CHP can be seen as placing their work within "context[s] of meaning" that more traditional schoolwork rarely engages; as helping, in turn, to strengthen or perpetuate these contexts; and, in the process, as enabling more such work in the future.

In the early years of the CHP, the *Chronicle-Tribune* ran annual articles featuring student work as well as intermittently announcing honors that the project had received. A feature article from New Year's Day 2002 provides an example of a successful project from the period. The headline places the student's work front and center: "David Blunk II is on a mission to find Samuel

Plato structures" (Smith, 2002). Plato, a prototypical "Marion Hero," was an African American architect responsible for some of Marion's most significant and beloved structures. As the newspaper article explains, "A research paper on Plato already existed"—the work of an earlier student—"but there weren't good photographs of his buildings. Munn knew David had an interest in photography, so he suggested the idea." Like students in many of the articles, Blunk is at once treated like a child—note the subtly dismissive use of his first name in the passage that follows—and cited as an authority:

> David said the Hostess House, 723 W. Fourth St., is Plato's best-known building, but he's found about a dozen structures by Plato.
>
> "The other prominent building is the First Baptist Church," David said. "And there's a lot more he's constructed that have not been wholly identified as his.
>
> Samuel Plato was the most prominent African-American architect for Grant County. He was really into the Arts & Crafts Movement. He was trained to be a cabinet-maker, and his buildings have high-quality design.
>
> The windows are a trademark of his." (Smith, 2002)

Blunk places Plato's work in cultural context, and he appears to correctly associate both Plato and the Arts and Crafts movement with craftsmanship and quality detailing (although this connection could admittedly be more explicit). The knowledge Blunk displays is specialized enough that it was presumably gained while working on the project, and while his statements can serve as proof of learning, they also come in the course of providing a public service—informing newspaper readers. The coverage provides the student—this one, at least—a taste of public recognition and an opportunity to think of himself as an expert who can use his learning to inform the public. In the article, Blunk goes on to explain his goals for the project:

> I'm going to do black-and-white photographs of all the buildings, then arrange them on the [CHP web page] and hopefully exhibit the photographs somewhere.... This idea allows me to do a historical project as well as an artistic project. I do like history, and I wanted to do something that would benefit Grant County. And this project will. (Smith, 2002)

The idea of learning as a public service could hardly be stated more clearly. Whether the work is more artistic or historical (or both) is open to debate. Clearly, it engaged historical knowledge, showed a practical application of the need for context, and raised the question of which buildings Samuel Plato had designed. Blunk produced a brief written introduction to his work, but it also seems likely that he spent a significant portion of project time composing and then developing photographs. Overall, though, this sort of work at least holds the potential for engaging interesting historical questions. True to Blunk's hopes, the photographs were exhibited at the Marion Public Library, at the Minnetrista Center in Muncie, and in a museum in Florida. They are now stored at the Marion Public Library along with professionally printed signs from the Muncie installation. When I visited the library in August 2011, Blunk's collection was again on display as a rotating exhibit.[6]

The *Chronicle-Tribune* reported on many similar projects during those years: In 1998, an article covered a student's documentary on the local Underground Railroad, occasioned by its screening before the members of the Grant County Historical Society (L. Robinson, 1998). In 1999, the newspaper publicized a student's website about the Miami Indian Cemetery north of town (Smith, 1999). In 2000, a web project about the Indiana Truck Company was featured (Sharma, 2000). The article from 2001 covered a variety of projects on Marion's historic structures (Waters, 2001a). At the center of these articles is the idea that students are creating products that, in a variety of ways, have value for the community. The 1999 article quotes the student who had researched the Miami Indian Cemetery, matching names with stones: "I think it makes it more worthwhile for other people to use it.... Research isn't any good unless someone else can use it" (Smith, 1999, p. A1). This has the ring of Munn's language, but it is encouraging to see it taken up and endorsed by a student. Some articles discuss the value of students' discoveries of new facts or of their work to document memories before they are gone. Others describe the artifacts created by students and detail their uses. The documentary, the *Chronicle-Tribune* notes, was being shown to area middle-schoolers (L. Robinson, 1998), and the articles invariably announce how the work would be made available.

Both newspaper coverage and Munn's final grant report cite, as a strength of the project, the personal connections made between students and interviewees (Munn, n.d.). A 2008 *Chronicle-Tribune* article highlights the way these developing relationships, in conjunction with the prospect of publication, help elicit strong student work:

> Justin Shockey... said being published made him want to do his best. He feels he's been able to leave a little piece of him behind as he moves on to college at Indiana University.

> "I was really excited about the idea that we'd get to publish it online," he said.
>
> But beyond personal motivations, Shockey said he didn't want to let down the man he profiled on the site, Gene Estle.
>
> "I wanted to make him proud when he read it," Shockey said. (Colley, 2008)

One might have supposed, by this point, that the chief value of the work would lie in its consumption by readers or in the students' learning, but this article suggests that interviewees can derive benefits as well. Another article from the era confirms this, saying, "The people interviewed were thrilled that someone cared to listen to them" (Waters, 2000).

There seems also to be an awareness that the research would help students to see the present-day city of Marion in a more historically informed way. Under the headline, "Students Uncover Area's Forgotten Past: Class Projects End Up on Library Website," Munn explains:

> "When I started thinking about black history in Grant County and the interactions between blacks and whites over the years, I realized we had a generation of students who didn't know Marion was a segregated city."
>
> Through old newspapers and other library sources, those effects are documented, Munn said. It was simply a matter of having students research the material. (Smith, 1999, p. A1)

One African American girl learned about "how racism affected her grandmother." An Asian American boy was told, by an interviewee, "how she became terrified when her family went out on a leisurely drive downtown and became trapped in the middle of an angry lynch mob" (in itself a provocative phrasing that should raise eyebrows). These historical experiences are far from the day-to-day concerns of most students, and the research makes them more immediate, showing them things that happened in the place where they live, to people with whom they can speak firsthand. In the same article, another student explains why these experiences matter. "The past shapes who we are," she says, adding, "You have to know your past" (Waters, 2000). There may be something of a platitude in this comment, but even a platitude can, if contemplated and reinterpreted in light of new experiences, lead to deeper understanding. With only a brief quote to work from, it is impossible to probe the depth of this student's thought—one reason I returned to study the process in action.

This string of newspaper articles speaks to the value of the CHP on multiple levels. First, the articles demonstrate public interest; reporters were sent year after year. There is a high degree of human interest in these pieces, which often but not always seem to be part of the "education beat," and administrators must have been delighted by the way they tell uplifting stories of service by local schools and students. Likewise, this press coverage must have added to the sense among students and subjects that their work mattered to the community. The articles also contain historical substance, although it should be said that any critical history is leavened with tributes to veterans and memories of streetcars, likely appealing both to the history buff and to the nostalgia of a town that had seen better days. The idea of nostalgia raises potential problems, which I address preliminarily below, but regardless, articles like these are not only *reflections* of value. By informing the public, they can *create* value. Finally, the attention helped to generate new research leads. Bill Munn explained to me that he used the articles to solicit reader ideas and artifacts like old photographs, and this use is also clear enough from the stories themselves, such as one that asks readers to notify Munn of rumored stations on the Underground Railroad (Smith, 2000).

Some newspaper items testify to the work's value more explicitly. A 1998 editorial, for example, praises the work as a source of value to both student and community. It reads, in part: "The Community History Project is providing an important service to the community. Bill Munn, the Marion High School social studies teacher who oversees the project, is not only helping preserve the area's history, he is also sharing the history with the students who are working with him on the project" ("Preservation as Progress," 1998). The editorial not only acknowledges a nontraditional community role for teacher, students, and school, but also reflects more traditional assumptions about learning. It is entirely appropriate to thank Munn, who initiated the project, but the students were more than mere recipients, and the history in these projects was shared as much by local citizens as by the teacher. The editors explain the project's value in a way that would be familiar to Bellah and colleagues (1985). The CHP's efforts, they say, "give us a record of where our city and our people have been, what they looked like and what they did" ("Preservation as Progress," 1998). The project received several awards—one from Compaq, another from the American Association for State and Local History—and each is reported in the newspaper, complete with laudatory testimonials (Waters, 1999, 2001b). Those closer to the situation were able to identify precise contributions made to the community's historical understanding. Barbara Love, the head of the public library's Indiana Room for local history, said, "I'm proudest of the films they've made. ... We give them out to teachers and anyone who is interested. This is just wonderful for high school students. Their research is so much in-depth they've found out things I didn't know" (Smith, 1999).

Another measure of the value of student work comes from its use, and some of the strongest evidence of this comes when it is cited in other publications. Madison references student-collected oral histories four times in his book on the Marion lynching—specifically, in his discussion of its aftermath in the 1930s and 1940s (Madison, 2001, p. 164, n.31, p. 178, n.1, p. 179, n.17, p. 180, n.43). Even more remarkable is a citation in Cynthia Carr's *Our Town* (2006). Carr's book tells of a 1970 episode in which Marion police allegedly responded with excessive violence to an attempted robbery by a local member of the Black Panthers. The *Chronicle-Tribune*, says Carr, claims that a police officer was shot in the hand by a sniper and quotes the city's first black chief of detectives to the effect that police had not fired a single shot. Carr heard rumors to the contrary, however, from both the Black Panther member himself and a member of the police force, so she attempted to investigate further:

> Jim Perkins, another African American on the police force in 1970, did not return my phone calls, but he'd been interviewed for the Community History Project, and there in his transcript at the Marion library was his recollection of that night: "The police shot that place up. There must have been 100 rounds that went through there." (Carr, 2006, p. 218)

The transcript came from a memorable 2001 project by Lucas White on segregation in Grant County. A white boy raised in part by an African American stepmother, Lucas White went well beyond the project requirements, interviewing six local African American elders and organizing quotations from the interviews by topic. It seems likely that his family relationships or his status as a local high school student helped open doors that were closed to a *Village Voice* reporter such as Carr; many CHP interviews develop in exactly this way. Whatever the explanation, the fact is that Lucas White, working through the CHP, procured an important piece of information and made it publicly accessible to later researchers. White's experience goes well beyond the ordinary, but there are many more consistently attainable ways in which students' work can be used and recognized—including, as I will explain, being cited by Munn in his public historical outreach.

Before moving to this final section, let me add one note of my own ambivalence. Munn emphasizes the critical aspects of the CHP, and they are real and substantial, but more often than not, the projects take a positive tone toward their subjects and the city, sometimes with the ring of nostalgia or boosterism. One unpublished project on a local menswear store shows both tendencies and reads like an advertisement: "In the early 1900s, customer and employee relationships meant a lot to the customer, and [the store] strove to have the best service in the city. They focused on treating their customers like family. Once a person would buy one item from [the store], the quick service and friendly attitude made the customer want to come back for another purchase." Sometimes, such projects serve goals that could be justified on strictly communitarian grounds. Projects on multicultural "heroes," positive in tone, draw attention to worthy figures who would otherwise be left out of town histories. In other cases, projects may have multiple layers of meaning, with the more critical ones partially camouflaged. For example, Munn has explained to me that he thinks the documentation of veterans' experiences draws attention to the horrors of war even as it honors service. Finally, positive projects may balance out or provide cover for more hard-hitting work. Relentless critique would likely compromise community support and might also raise issues of academic freedom in the high school, casting in a new light the issue of teacher tenure.

Whatever redeeming values nostalgia and boosterism might have for the city and the CHP, from the perspective of students' intellectual development they can be regarded as a weakness of the project. Students' historical understanding would be better served by participation in more rigorous forms of discourse, and future efforts such as the CHP would do well to develop methods that discourage boosterism and better reconcile the goals of critique and community building. This is a concern that informs the remainder of the study. Because the 2011 project involves a lynching, the threat of nostalgia is less pronounced than it might otherwise have been, but there is a parallel possibility that the project would create a similarly uncritical glorification of a present-day Marion, free from racism. This seems likely to be an enduring sort of dilemma, precisely because it shows how a project can create value in some respects while compromising others that are important to the discipline of history and the academic curriculum.

Bill Munn goes public

Through his leadership of the CHP, Bill Munn took on an expanded public role. Munn had long been a civically engaged teacher, knowledgeable in his field, but as the project progressed, he developed into a new role as Marion's leading public historian. His knowledge of local history deepened, he developed a personal historical agenda, and he assumed positions from which to better serve the community and demonstrate the public value of learning. It would be too much to say that Munn's pedagogical experiments caused this evolution. Many of the seeds of this later innovation were present in Munn's early work, and any causation must run in multiple directions. Still, the founding of the CHP marked a turning point in his career. Afterward, his research, his teaching, and his students' work all became more public, and knowledge gained through his teaching activities was vital to his community outreach.

Upon the founding of the project in 1997, looking back over the two years of experiments leading up to that point, Munn told the *Chronicle-Tribune*, "I really have to confess my local history was not strong" (Smith, 1997). Even if this was self-deprecating modesty, his projects and writings through 1997 and beyond show undeniable learning. Munn built on the information students uncovered, sometimes assigning them to later students for follow-up, and at other times tracking down leads himself (Smith, 1999). For one stretch of time, he documented the work of a local, early twentieth-century political cartoonist, working under a grant from the Indiana Humanities Council and Indiana Historical Society. During another, he began a campaign to replace the World War I plaque on the courthouse lawn, on which African American soldiers were marked (COL.) for "colored" (Shaw, 2000).

Munn's most enduring interest was in showing that African Americans in Marion have a past that is accessible to research. In 1998, he began formulating a project that would help him develop research skills in African American genealogy and family history, assess the difficulty of such work, and determine what sorts of research would be feasible for students to carry out. In many cases, African American histories in Grant County begin with the town of Weaver, an African American community that once flourished in a rural area just south of Marion. During the 1998–1999 school year, two students researched and produced a documentary video about the erstwhile community, and another student interviewed an African American elder, Irene Beck, who was descended from Weaverites (Wright, 1999). Munn began to develop a sense that, contrary to popular belief, black family histories could be traced, and that a group of people often regarded as without a history could reclaim one. He cites as influences a number of books that came out before and during this research—especially Edward Ball's *Slaves in the Family* (1998) and Scott

Malcomson's *One Drop of Blood* (2001)—which showed the line between black and white America to be more fluid than was commonly understood.

As he searched, Munn became captivated by an 1884 obituary in the *Marion Weekly Chronicle*, which said of the departed Matthew Becks:

> For fifty years the old man lived as a slave. Forty-four years he lived a free man with no master but his Maker. Since his freedom from slavery he paid $1,500 for his wife and children. He was a worthy and valuable citizen, owing nothing when he died, and was the father of six or eight robust sons, who are honest, industrious men. His life was honorable and profitable to his country. (Wright, 1999)

Munn applied for and received a $7,500 fellowship from the Lilly Endowment to follow Becks's trail on the grounds that this would provide a model of research on African American history that would benefit both his students and the public. Munn visited Becks's point of origin in southwestern Virginia and then ventured to Boston, where Becks lived with the abolitionist William Lloyd Garrison and spoke to his followers. After consulting with Garrison's biographer, Henry Mayer, and perusing every issue of Garrison's newspaper, *The Liberator*, Munn found a reference to Becks in the final issue.

Munn has presented this research but never published it. As he continually reminds me, he is not much of a bookkeeper, and there are still files unread from that research trip. In his retirement, however, Munn hopes to find time to publish the work, perhaps in the *Indiana Magazine of History*. In the meantime, this research gave him a greater familiarity with issues in research on African American history and then spurred further investigations. In 2007, as their semester project, Munn and about a third of his students restored the cemetery at Weaver. (Other students undertook more typical projects, such as oral history interviews—an arrangement that resembles the organization of our 2011 lynching research.) A professional cemetery restorer donated his time, working with students on Saturday mornings and for two weeks after school had ended to finish the job. For their individual portions of the project, each student researched a single headstone, reconstructing brief biographies that remain on file at the public library. Munn tells of how he and the students were hosted for breakfast each morning by one neighbor, and of how other local residents would visit the work party and embrace the students. One neighbor recalled watching out his window on the night of the lynching as the body of Thomas Shipp was lowered into an unmarked grave. Speaking with Munn and the students, he identified the exact spot of the burial, which had until that point gone undocumented.

Over this period, Munn himself began to assume a more prominent public role. Beginning in 1997, he wrote a series of history columns for the *Chronicle-Tribune*—more than fifty, by my count—many of which drew on student research. The columns eventually tapered off, but in recent years he has been a regular guest on morning radio, where he presents a weekly segment on Grant County history and periodically mentions student work. In 2008, he was named official Grant County Historian by the Indiana Historical Society, and shortly thereafter, the *Chronicle-Tribune* printed a letter to the editor from the provost of Marion's Indiana Wesleyan University, Jerry Pattengale, a white man who happens to live in the area once known as Weaver. "A few years ago, I benefited directly in my research from attending his work in Weaver, restoring the African-American cemetery with some of his students.... Thanks, Bill for being both a teacher to traditional students as well as to older educators like myself" (Pattengale, 2008). Pattengale, trained as a historian, cites the project as a historical source in a personal reflection on Weaver in his college-level textbook, *The Purpose-Guided Student* (2010, p. 76, n. 3). In 2011, I interviewed Pattengale, asking him to conduct a closer reading of the students' projects on the Marion lynching. This is reported in Chapter 5.

At the state level, Munn served from 2003 to 2005 on the editorial board of the *Indiana Magazine of History*. In one issue of the magazine, he dipped a toe into the academic conversation, in the process making explicit some of the rationale for his community history work. In that issue, the journal ran an essay by Indiana University historian David Thelen, in which Thelen argues that "re-enactment" or "re-experiencing" of historical events, broadly understood, restores their open-endedness—the possibility that they might have played out differently, if different decisions had been made (Thelen, 2003). In his response, Munn endorses Thelen's goal of restoring agency to history, linking this to the 1960s social studies injunction to "open up the closed areas" of history and society (Crumrin, Bunch, & Munn, 2003, p. 167). But he gently yet forcefully probes the limitations of re-enactment, asking, "Would the audience sit still for a re-enactment of the Nat Turner revolt, the Pullman strike, or the Marion lynching?" (Crumrin et al., 2003, p. 168) Munn argues for the "opening" power of traditional tools of historical inquiry and instruction, like documentary analysis and Socratic seminars, especially when they are applied as a part of real historical inquiry. He then goes on:

> I have had success with students interviewing older community members of the World War II generation for an oral history project. Students then presented their work to

> fellow students, community members, and to the subjects and their families. I recall a student interview of a former POW who had spent two years in a German prison camp. At the end of the student presentation, the man was given a very tearful standing ovation. Another student interviewed a group of older African Americans about their experiences growing up in a segregated Marion, Indiana. There was total silence in the group when the humiliations endured by the folks were recounted. I believe that the connection that Thelen describes was made. (Crumrin et al., 2003, p. 169)

The evidence I gathered in Munn's classroom serves, in part, to evaluate this sort of claim and assess the extent to which community history research facilitates connections at the same level that one might expect of a re-enactment, if not of the same exact character.

Figure 2: Glass Factory, Marion, Indiana, October 1908.
One of three and possibly four photographs taken by Lewis Wickes Hine in the glass factories of Marion. Hine's caption read: "Bill, a carrying-in boy, Canton Glass Works, Marion, Ind. Gets $.80 a day or night. Others below fourteen, too. Location: Marion, Indiana." (Library of Congress, Prints & Photographs Division, National Child Labor Committee Collection, LC-DIG-nclc-01205)

One U.S. history lesson, unrelated to the lynching project, answers in the affirmative while also showing the long-term fruits of CHP research. In April 2011, during my second week back in Marion, I sat in the corner of Mr. Munn's classroom, its lights dimmed. A photograph, projected in front of the class, showed a factory scene and an adolescent boy working at some indeterminate manual task (see Figure 2). Munn did not identify the photograph immediately, but I recognized it as the work of Lewis Hine, the crusading Progressive Era photographer whose images fueled the campaign against child labor. The students looked on, following Munn's instructions to "read the photograph as a text" and writing down details and provisional interpretations. He cycled through two similar photographs and then returned to the first. "How old would you say the boy is? Where do you think this is?" The students guessed—Chicago? Detroit? New York? No, Munn replied, Marion. With an audible gasp, the students exclaimed, nearly in unison, "Marion!?" A class discussion ensued, as students analyzed details of the photograph and Munn provided contextual information about the boys' lives and Marion's glass factories. To gauge the class reaction, I checked in with three students from the lynching project who were sitting closest to me, and all three said the lesson was unusually interesting: the first student because it pertained to Marion, the second because it used images, and the third because his father worked in one of those factories. This lesson is the fruit of years of research. Munn discovered the photo in a Library of Congress collection, and student oral histories, such as a 1999 interview with a man who had worked in the factories as a child, helped him place it into context.[7] The work was reported in a 1999 *Chronicle-Tribune* article (Smith, 1999), and Munn wrote about it separately in his newspaper column (2000).

Discussion

On the strength of this varied work, and in light of its differences from common pedagogical practice, I judged that the CHP had something to contribute, not only to Marion but also to a strand within curriculum theory and history education. Even as I felt its appeal in a personal way, I saw as well an opportunity to look more closely, to test its assumptions, and to explore its limits. I have already mentioned one potential shortcoming of this sort of community-directed historical work: a tendency toward nostalgia and boosterism. In the further interest of balance, having just discussed some of the CHP's most notable successes, let me add two additional observations on those limits. First, although the project shows, in some ways, a great deal of attention to students' interests, not every mention of local history is as successful as the one on the glass factory, and there are times when the topics seem more meaningful to Munn than to the students—something akin to the stereotypical college professor, teaching in the areas of his or her own specialized research. As teachers develop intellectual agendas and identities, this may be a predictable result.

Second, when the classroom is opened to value-producing work and, inevitably, to value judgments, questions will arise about what to do when teacher and student values conflict. This has been a relatively minor issue in the CHP. Munn's political leanings are no secret, and they may prompt occasional grumbling, but the classroom is not highly politicized. Students are given considerable leeway to choose research topics and formulate arguments, and the project assignments, to the extent that they serve potentially political ends, such as the elevation of multicultural heroes or the documentation of war experiences, do so in relatively unobjectionable ways. If a project were to undertake more critical history, as I have suggested would be desirable, this issue could become more salient. This also raises questions about how student work is to be evaluated. In this research, I seek judgments from a variety of perspectives including from members of the public and the students themselves—a method that, I think, captures the complexities of real-world evaluation better than the artificial simplicity of a standard grading scale. This should hardly be the last word on the subject, but it raises more questions—about the value of grading when public values are also at issue—than I am able to answer at present.

Conclusion

Bill Munn's approach to teaching sits squarely within a progressive, project-based tradition, and yet it also goes well beyond typical classroom practice, especially in its community orientation, in its intellectual sophistication, and in the cumulative effect of a project sustained over many years. I have provided, I hope, a sense of the excitement of the work itself, the range of past student projects, and where our work in 2011 fit among them. Projects such as David Blunk's and Lucas White's show how a process of cultural production might result in learning for both the student and community, a relationship explored at greater length in the following chapter. The various projects also suggest different ways in which both students and teacher have come to terms with the world they have inherited—a process through which they have worked out, in light of their community's history and their own interests and capacities, how best they can contribute and what sorts of projects they should undertake.

In a community like Marion, it may be most natural to think of historical inheritance in primarily negative terms. The history of race in the United States can be seen as a sort of secular equivalent of original sin, where the world into which we are born—and the culture that forms us—are inescapably shot through with injustice and prejudice. The Marion lynching has been interpreted in these terms: At the end of the lynching project, Munn was contacted regarding the students' work by a Milwaukee independent screenwriter shopping a James Cameron biopic entitled *Fruit of the Tree*. Doubtless, such an interpretation of history is sometimes appropriate. However, the writer Marilynne Robinson presents an alternative in her novel *Gilead*, which concerns, in part, a nineteenth-century, anti-slavery crusader who moved to John Brown's Kansas to "make himself useful to the cause of abolition" (2004, p. 49). For Robinson, our heritage is not only negative. Invoking the theological notion of "prevenient grace," she views us as inheriting and inhabiting a world filled with "more beauty than our eyes can bear," in which "precious things have been put into our hands and to do nothing to honor them is to do great harm" (2004, p. 246). This, I think, approximates Bill Munn's vision of history, in which both great injustice and powerful tools have been handed down. As I understand Munn's work, it is the tools placed into his hands—by the abolitionists and transcendentalists, the pragmatists and progressives, the theologians and the student activists—that at once obligate and strengthen him to do justice to the past.

· 2 ·

LEARNING-AS-A-SERVICE

> Every method which appeals to the child's active powers, to his capacities in construction, production, and creation, marks an opportunity to shift the center of ethical gravity from an absorption which is selfish to a service which is social.
>
> —John Dewey (1903, p. 17)

The assumptions reflected in the CHP stand out against the current educational landscape, but they are not without precedent. This chapter places them in the context of a long, primarily Deweyan tradition and sets out a rationale for investigating the public value of students' work products. There has been a tendency in recent thought and practice, even among Dewey's heirs, to regard these work products as externalized indications of capacities for thinking and understanding that are the property of individual learners. Occasionally, they are taken as cognitive achievements shared among members of a classroom learning community. I would like to draw attention to another possibility: of considering those work products in terms of the values they create for others—the ways in which they edify, entertain, enlighten, or prove otherwise useful—especially for audiences outside the school. Of course, it will always remain important to consider the capacities that students develop through this work. It is in the public interest, most would agree, to see that young citizens develop skills, habits, and values necessary to sustain a democratic society. Such a society also typically affirms the legitimate pursuit of personal interests, subject to some constraints, and I assume that there is a place for learners to pursue these interests as well. However, by conceiving of learning as creative activity taking place within a shared culture that stretches beyond the school, and by evaluating learning based on the educational values that it produces in that broad context, we can engage students in considering the social implications of their learning and thereby heighten its felt significance.

To explain what is meant by "public value" will eventually require touching upon Dewey's philosophical writings of the late 1920s and 1930s (and then examining the pedagogy in action, in chapters to come), but the basic idea is already present—and is expressed in what is probably its most familiar form—in Dewey's turn-of-the-century educational writings. In his 1903 *Ethical Principles Underlying Education*, Dewey invited readers to consider the typical schools of the day:

> Imagine forty children all engaged in reading the same books, and in preparing and reciting the same lessons day after day. Suppose that... they are continually judged from the standpoint of what they are able to take in in a study hour, and to reproduce in a recitation hour. (1903, p. 15)

Replace recitation with standardized testing, and it requires little imagination to see how this passage speaks to the current situation as well as Dewey's own, especially with regard to the uniformity of the curricular program and the imitative rather than creative character of the learning. Dewey finds this curricular model—of learning as reproduction—to be wanting. When all students are asked to reproduce the same knowledge, he writes, "There is no opportunity for each child to work out something specifically his own, which he may contribute to the common stock, while he, in turn, participates in the productions of others" (Dewey, 1903, p. 16). This brief passage suggests at least three points of critique: First, and most important for present purposes, students' work products in such a classroom make no social contribution. Second, because of this, the students have limited opportunity to develop personal strengths or unique roles within the group. Third, because students are being judged based on their performance on identical tasks, they have reason to see each other as competitors rather than collaborators.[1]

In *The School and Society* (1899), Dewey describes a very different sort of learning environment, and the contrast between the two can stand as a sort of thought experiment. Here, he conjures a stylized preindustrial scene and asks readers to consider how, in an era before compulsory formal schooling, children learned what they needed to get by in the world. In these homes and communities, he proposes, there was always work to be done—sheep to shear, clothes to sew, candles to make, and crops to grow. Children were motivated to help with these tasks because they "really needed to be done" in order for the household to function. If the tasks were not completed—if clothing and food went unmade—people would go cold and hungry. As a result, children participated in work that was "of immediate and personal concern," with "a real motive behind and a real outcome ahead" (Dewey, 1899, pp. 8–9) and that thus held their attention and demanded their quality effort.

To this sort of consequential work, Dewey attributes a number of educational benefits that are at once ethically and intellectually charged. It provides "training in habits of order and industry, and in the idea of responsibility, of obligation to do something, to produce something, in the world" (1903, p. 8). He claims, as well, that it helps to cultivate the sort of cooperative character necessary for democratic life in the urban industrial society that was then emerging. If a goal is meaningful and children can accomplish it better with each other's help, they will work together, "not for the sake of the sharing, but for the sake of the product" (1903, p. 8). Cooperation is best learned not as an isolated skill, but as a part of the meaningful, value-creating activities that make it advantageous. In much the same way, productive work offers opportunities to introduce children to academic subject matter. In Dewey's conception, activity in the academic disciplines addresses persistent human needs, just as the household chores seen above, but it does so in more complex ways that have been developed and refined over time. A skilled teacher sees the connections between the two, channeling students' desires into work activities and guiding them in progressively more sophisticated thought and practice (Dewey, 1902). (Of course, what counts as "more sophisticated" is up for debate, so this deceptively simple formulation masks some of the most challenging questions of the method.)

Most of the curricular examples Dewey provides pertain to elementary education and ask students to perform tasks such as cooking and gardening that serve others within the classroom or school community.[2] In *Schools of To-Morrow*, a survey of progressive curricular experiments written with his daughter Evelyn, there are indications of what this sort of instruction might look like with older students, benefiting not only fellow students but also the surrounding community (Dewey & Dewey, 2008). The Deweys liken an Indianapolis high school to a settlement house, akin to Jane Addams's Hull House, that enriches its urban neighborhood. They also highlight a "pure milk campaign" in Gary, Indiana, where "pupils brought samples of milk from home and tested it, and then saw that their parents did something about it if impurities were found" (2008, p. 109). In the course of pursuing pressing social needs, students came to participate in purposeful scientific practice.

Ted Sizer and the exhibition movement

Through the years, Deweyan ideas have been adapted and reinterpreted for a great many new contexts and demands. The modern reform era, from the 1980s to the present, has been overwhelmingly concerned with academic achievement and assessment, and one of the most prominent progressive educators of that era, Ted Sizer, showed how students' productive activities can play a role in the assessment process, preserving some measure of respect for the complexity of learning and of students' intellectual lives. There is much to admire in Sizer's life and work. His program of reform was deeply humane and democratic, and it made room for a level of creativity not commonly seen in other reforms of the era. Bill Munn's CHP was made possible, in part, by Sizer's "exhibition movement" and by the practice of performance assessment developed by Sizer's protégé, Grant Wiggins. However, while these approaches to assessment are far preferable to dominant forms of standardized assessment, they give short shrift to the Deweyan insight that such products can be of value not only for what they say about students but also for how they enrich the lives of audience members and the public at large.

Sizer's best-known work, *Horace's Compromise*, surveyed the state of U.S. high schools in the early 1980s. Based on hundreds of observations in a cross section of schools, Sizer concluded that a disheartening number of students were merely going through the motions, working toward superficial indicators rather than real learning:

> Most students see the *diploma* as their high school goal, the passport to their next stage of life. The way to receive it, they now know, is to serve time, to be in attendance the requisite number of weeks in the requisite courses. One thereby amasses "credits," which ultimately "earn" the diploma. *Attendance* is the way it is done. (1984, p. 63, emphasis in original)

In an effort to combat this sort of empty credentialism, Sizer called for tightening the link between certificates, assessments, and desired student competencies. He proposed that diplomas should not reward mere attendance but should be awarded "only when there is a clear exhibition by the student that such learning has been mastered" (Sizer, 1984, p. 63). Sizer thus calls his proposed assessments "exhibition[s] of mastery," a phrase deliberately chosen because it conveys the way in which they provide students with the "opportunity to show off" what they have learned (1984, p. 68). The self-centeredness of this phrase, "show off," is startling, especially when contrasted with Dewey's desire to see productive activity as a way to move students from an "absorption which is selfish to a service which is social" (1903, p. 17).[3] Selfishness, it should be said, is hardly the defining characteristic of Sizer's reform agenda. Indeed, the phrase strikes something of a false note amid a book and larger body of work marked by deep civic-mindedness and moral concern (see also Sizer & Sizer, 2000). Sizer's choice of words is revealing, however, for what it says about the primary role of students' work products in the exhibition system: to "display" or "demonstrate" their learning (Sizer, 1992, pp. 12, 62).

Sizer's follow-up book, *Horace's School*, offers examples of what exhibitions might look like, all of which provide opportunities to display learning. Students might recite a speech or draw a map from memory; repair a deliberately "sabotaged" vehicle; or write an extended essay on a passage from a Supreme Court decision and explain its relevance to a "hypothetical" new case. Reflecting Sizer's Deweyan sensibility, some of the proposed exhibitions do also make contributions to family or school communities. Students might work in groups to complete their family's tax returns—a real-world task in which failure is a federal offense, even if the motivational value is otherwise dubious—or to develop healthy menus for the school cafeteria to demonstrate their knowledge of nutrition. Many others do not, however, like a decidedly inward-looking project in which a student would "*select a human emotion, examine it from a variety of disciplinary perspectives, and prepare a portfolio that explores the emotion through an essay and three other forms of expression*" (Sizer, 1992, pp. 23, 48, 65, 98–99, 118). The common aspiration of Sizerian exhibitions is not that they perform a service for others but that they demonstrate student mastery. Such a process may motivate students' quality work through accountability, but the projects do not produce public value in the same sense as, for example, Dewey's pure milk campaign. Thus, Sizer underplays one of Dewey's key insights, in which productive learning is more a matter of *contribution* than *exhibition*.

Understanding by Design

Sizer's work gave rise to the Coalition of Essential Schools, a significant reform movement of the 1980s and 1990s and a network of progressive schools that includes, at the time of this writing, some six hundred exhibition-oriented member institutions. The influence of his exhibition movement is also felt, with perhaps even greater currency, in the idea of performance assessment and in the Understanding by Design (UbD) framework for curriculum planning, which were developed by the Coalition's former director of research, Grant Wiggins, and, in the latter case, his collaborator Jay McTighe. As with Sizer, UbD foregrounds the role of assessment in the curriculum planning process. Wiggins and McTighe call for teachers, when developing curricular units, to first "think like an assessor," clearly articulating the "enduring understandings" and skills that are the goal of a curricular unit and then determining what evidence would be necessary to show that goals have been met—what "performances" students should be expected to provide to demonstrate that the understandings have been achieved (Wiggins & McTighe, 2005, pp. 148, 128, 17). In theory, competence could be demonstrated through "ephemeral" performances, but Wiggins and McTighe say that an effective performance assessment "typically involves the creation of products" that can be preserved and reviewed by outsiders (2005, p. 346). Once performance goals have been established, a teacher would set about "backwards designing" the unit (Wiggins & McTighe, 2005, p. 13), planning a sequence of activities that would prepare students to provide the requisite proof of learning.[4]

Performances in UbD function similarly to Sizer's exhibitions, and the two systems have similar strengths and limitations.[5] To Wiggins's and McTighe's credit (and in a highly Deweyan vein), performances require students to provide visible evidence of learning and to put their understandings into practice in the world. Wiggins and McTighe are especially concerned to tease out various "facets of understanding," which they consistently define in terms of observable behaviors (e.g., Can the student explain an idea thoroughly? Provide examples or make generalizations? Formulate interpretations, analogies, or narratives that show its significance?) (Wiggins & McTighe, 2005, chap. 4). Yet as with Sizer, these preeminent goals of learning are conceived as capacities, skills, or understandings belonging to individual learners, and products or performances are interpreted as pointing back to the learner and demonstrating the degree to which he or she has met learning goals.

Contrary to this assumption, performances and productive activities can have many goals besides giving rise to individual skills or understandings on the part of the actor or creator. They can serve to edify, entertain, and enlighten audience members and even, by so doing, to effect broader social change. Likewise, products themselves can be interpreted as more than externalized, persistent representations of student capacities. They can, for example, provide audience members with experiences of beauty, alleviate hunger or sickness, or remedy historical injustices. It may be the case that schools have a special responsibility for cultivating student understandings, but even those understanding goals typically include students' valuing of what is being learned, and that value is bound up in the learning's social uses and purposes and in the anticipated valuings of others.

In Bill Munn's CHP, an audience member might read a student's local history project, learn about the history of the community, value the project for what it taught her (the audience member), and also appreciate the thoughtfulness and historical insight it demonstrated on the part of the student, a potential future civic leader. The student, in turn, might think the project worthwhile because it educated others, advanced an argument of some importance in the world, and helped him (the student) to see his community in a new way. The learning and valuing of the producer and consumer here are each dependent on the full experience of the other. If the student were to create an artifact knowing that only the teacher would read it—or knowing that it would be read by community members, but that they would approach it as an examination rather than a learning opportunity—then the student would likely imagine the reader's experience differently and by extension approach the writing task differently. The student might still take the opportunity to practice a writing technique or develop some personal knowledge, but these would be experienced and constructed differently in the absence of an opportunity to create value through what he creates.[6]

For Sizer, Wiggins, and McTighe, the curriculum process begins with questions like "What should students understand and be able to do?" or "What should they exhibit?" These questions merit consideration, but a process that accounts for the public value of students' work products would also ask, in collaboration with students, "What should we contribute?" Later in the learning process, when student work products were examined, it would be important to assess not only the mastery they demonstrate on the part of the creator but also the value that the work has created for the reader and others—and, in light of the experience, to discuss what would be valuable to undertake next.

Foxfire

Another progressive curricular experiment, roughly contemporary to Sizer's work, provides some indication of what it might look like to learn and assess in this way. Based in the foothills of rural north Georgia, *Foxfire* began life as a high school literary magazine but came to specialize in documenting the folk culture of southern Appalachia. Students interviewed elderly rural residents and documented their agricultural practices, religious rituals, musical techniques, and other traditional folkways (Puckett, 1989). (Thus, *Foxfire* is of special interest because it covers similar thematic ground to the CHP.) The magazine built a subscription base beyond the school, and in 1972 a collection of its articles was published by Doubleday as *The Foxfire Book* (Wigginton, 1972). The work was favorably reviewed in numerous major media outlets including the *New York Times*, and it became a surprise popular hit, topping the *New York Times* Best Sellers list in its first month. Royalties averaged $100,000 annually for the first five years, and a total of nine *Foxfire* books were published in the 1970s and 1980s. The project inspired a Broadway play, a *Hallmark Hall of Fame* movie, and hundreds of similar projects across the country (Puckett, 1989).[7]

Foxfire's reception stands as an example of what must be the upper bounds of the public value that student projects can create. The most thorough appraisal of the project was carried out by educational researcher John L. Puckett (1989), and one of the most important lessons of Puckett's text is that such a program can create value (or fall short) in many different ways—including with reference to its effects on students, collaborators, and audience members—and that it will necessarily be judged by a range of interested parties who employ varying standards and criteria of value. In judging the success of the project for its national audience, Puckett counts the sales figures, spinoffs, and reviews as positive evidence. He finds that the project created a great deal of value for its native region as well, spurring economic development in its home county and affirming the dignity of a region often derided as backward. The program was revered by most locals and especially by its elderly interviewees, who were gratified to learn that others were interested in them and their stories.

There was one audience among which *Foxfire* was less well received: practitioners of academic folklore. Richard Dorson, of Indiana University's Folklore Institute, was highly critical, accusing *Foxfire* of manufacturing what he called "fakelore" and alleging that, by publishing the work of untrained teachers and students, the project was engaged in "mis-education" of the public (quoted in Puckett, 1989, p. 48, n. 4). Another disciplinarian charged that *Foxfire*'s method of presenting interviews—highly edited and transcribed in exaggerated dialect—presented a romanticized, nostalgic version of the past, "packaging a consumer version of folk culture designed for a mass culture, middle-class, mostly white audience" (cited in Puckett, 1989, p. 267). If, as I have suggested, the reading of student work can involve not only inspection but also consequential learning on the part of the reader and impact on the larger culture, then it is important to note that this also carries risks, and that critiques can themselves be a source of learning.

The researcher, Puckett, also evaluates *Foxfire* in terms of students' personal learning and concludes that it helped build self-confidence, interpersonal skills, and a sense of their own cultural identity. He is less sanguine about the program's academic results and suggests that the program sometimes focused on magazine production to the detriment of student learning. The academic curriculum was often cast aside in order to satisfy, in Puckett's words, "the pressures of assembling a professional-quality magazine by quarterly printing and mailing deadlines" (1989, p. 79). Further, Wigginton and other adults played an active role in editing students' work, in ways that were often reasonable but sometimes bordered on dishonesty. (Investigating one of the magazine's signature pieces, Puckett finds an early draft entirely in Wigginton's handwriting.) In surveys of alumni, relatively few credited the program with improving their compositional skills, and a surprising number struggled with college writing.

Alongside the curricular approaches reviewed above, *Foxfire* can be seen as illustrating a set of possibilities within a product-oriented tradition. The project, and Puckett's evaluation of it, shows the complexity of goals for such work, notably students' personal and academic development and the public value created. Puckett does cast some doubt upon the academic results of the program and shows the risk of emphasizing products and production deadlines at the expense of students' personal learning. At the same time, *Foxfire* provides a useful counterpoint to Sizer and Wiggins, in that it demonstrates that student projects can make real, socially valued contributions and that this kind of learning can yield personal rewards for the creators.

Service-learning

Two other pedagogical approaches are worthy of brief discussion, both of which place special importance on students' productive activity: service-learning and project-based learning. Service-learning is explicitly rooted in the assumptions of Deweyan pragmatism (Eyler & Giles, 1999), and among active educational movements, it best carries forward the practice of learning through creating value for others. As the name suggests, scholarly literature in the field places social contribution on roughly equal footing with participants' personal growth. Indeed, one of the field's canonical documents, Sigmon's "Service-Learning: 3 Principles," admonishes that all service-learning must benefit the recipient of service as well as the learner and that learning objectives should be "formed in the context of what needs to be done to serve others" (1979, p. 10). If anything, service is sometimes given pride of place, to the point that it has become a common refrain to ask, "Where's the learning in service-learning?" (Eyler & Giles, 1999). In projects susceptible to this criticism, students might parachute into a service situation, perform some discrete action such as ladling soup, and then leave as quickly as they arrived, learning little about the nuances of the situation or the social and historical contexts in which their work is meaningful (Manley, Buffa, Dube, & Reed, 2006).

I have no major quarrel with the way service-learning is conceptualized, but it is unfortunate that it remains so peripheral to the academic work that dominates students' school days. This book aims to identify the service potential within more traditional academic subject matter—the activities through which the disciplines satisfy persistent human needs—and then to create ways for students to engage in this work. Many would hesitate, I think, to count the writing of scientific papers, or book reviews, or works of literary criticism as acts of service-learning, but work of this kind can make profound contributions and deserves to be incorporated into the curriculum. Instead of *service-learning*, this sort of learning might be called *learning-as-a-service*. In such a curricular approach, community needs would be prominent, and student work could address them, investigating the social roots of issues such as, say, poverty or public health disparities. However, student work would not be limited to ameliorating the most pressing social problems. Instead, it would be open to the full spectrum of human needs and values—I have in mind, for example, the quest for historical self-understanding—and would help students to address these needs in ways informed by existing communities of inquiry and practice.

Project-based learning

The curriculum project has been associated with Deweyan and progressive education for most of the life of that movement, and it remains a live option today. In the early years, the "project method" was pioneered by William Heard Kilpatrick, who interpreted Deweyan ideas for popular professional audiences. Kilpatrick defined the project as "wholehearted purposeful activity proceeding in a social environment" (1918, p. 4) and advocated for integrative curriculum that crossed disciplinary boundaries. In this, Kilpatrick resembles Wigginton and *Foxfire* more than Sizer or Wiggins and McTighe.

Project-based learning (PBL), its most notable contemporary incarnation, is more discipline based and academic. Two leading scholars of the subject, Krajcik and Blumenfeld, identify PBL research as having "refined and elaborated Dewey's original insight that active inquiry results in deeper understanding" (2006, p. 318). Krajcik and Blumenfeld synthesize this research, encapsulating the method in a series of principles. For example, students should formulate "driving questions," with teachers' assistance, and then engage, collaboratively, in "processes of problem solving that are central to expert performance in the discipline" (Krajcik & Blumenfeld, 2006, p. 318). It is their final principle, however, that is of greatest interest here: "Students create a set of tangible products that address the driving question. These are shared artifacts—publicly accessible external representations of the class's learning" (Krajcik & Blumenfeld, 2006, p. 318). Work products, they say, serve multiple functions in the learning process. They allow teachers to assess complex, high-level understandings—the idea championed by Wiggins and McTighe. They also serve as material representations of ideas, which students can "actively manipulate" in the process of forming understandings (Krajcik & Blumenfeld, 2006, p. 327). This sort of justification bears the imprint of constructionism, a line of inquiry based on Seymour Papert's conjecture that learners construct their own knowledge and that "this happens especially felicitously in a context where the learner is consciously engaged in constructing a public entity" (Papert, 1991, p. 1). Constructionism has focused on the idea that artifacts can serve as "objects to think with," just as the manipulation of physical gears of different sizes once helped a young Papert to grasp intuitively the concept of multiplication (Papert, 1980, p. 11).

Finally, Krajcik and Blumenfeld say, public artifacts allow students to "make their understandings visible to others" and available for "review" and "critique," which "permit[s] learners to reflect on and revise their work" (2006, p. 327), all arguments that draw on ideas from Brown and Campione's "community of learners" (1994) and Scardamalia and Bereiter's "knowledge-building communities" (2006). Brown and Campione regard knowledge not as something acquired by individual minds but as constructed by communities in the form of shared concepts, texts, and material artifacts. Scardamalia and Bereiter situate these calls in the context of a "larger societal knowledge building effort" (2006, p. 98) and argue that schools should induct students into that effort. These last programs draw increasingly close to the work of Bill Munn and the CHP and to the subject matter of this book. As it has developed, though, knowledge-building research attempts to formalize an intra-classroom process of "idea improvement" (Scardamalia, 2002) and then to develop a piece of software, Knowledge Forum, that structures students' activity according to that process. The theory is highly and perhaps overly prescriptive with regard to classroom processes and then, surprisingly, neglects the relationship of that work to the larger society. As a result, examples tend to show students operating on a sense of intellectual curiosity (e.g., Why do leaves change color?) and then replicating the work of others (Scardamalia, 2002). For example, Scardamalia and Bereiter are pleased to hear a fifth-grade knowledge-building student who is studying genetics remark that "Mendel worked on Karen's problem" rather than "Karen rediscovered Mendel" or "Karen should read Mendel to find the answer to her problem" (2006, p. 98). It is indeed encouraging that students would see themselves as legitimate participants in ongoing inquiry, but it is also hard to escape the feeling that there is some truth in the latter two statements.

I do not mean to suggest that there is no place for children to engage in this sort of inquiry, which seems to give them an active role in constructing knowledge and to encourage them to take responsibility for their own learning. If, however, the theory aims to capture the place of knowledge building in society, then it needs to engage students in work in which they have something real to contribute—if not at the very frontiers of scientific research then by formulating locally significant knowledge and by putting it into action in meaningful contexts. Personal curiosity can motivate inquiry, but so can the impulse to act—to address social needs, make an original contribution, or realize one's vision in the world. Deweyan inquiry is substantially a matter of action and concerns issues of value intertwined with those of fact (Joas, 1997, 2000; Putnam, 2002). What research on PBL and knowledge building leaves undone, and what I aim to do here, is to focus attention on the value of students' work products to the world outside the classroom. By developing this aspect of the project to a greater extent, I hope to strengthen this vital mode of learning.

Dewey and value

In early works, like those cited at the beginning of this chapter, Dewey frequently speaks of values, and he consistently attends to learning as it occurs through activity in social contexts. However, the nature of value and its relationship with action remain implicit or go unexplored. Drawing on Dewey's later work, scholars have filled in the picture somewhat by piecing together insights from Dewey's disparate writings on religion, art, public discourse, and value itself, but even in those writings the theory is not developed systematically.[8] As Gouinlock notes in the most comprehensive study of Deweyan value theory available (1972), Dewey does not always use terms and concepts consistently across these works, and any interpreter must make decisions about which usages and meanings to prioritize. I do not attempt to offer a definitive account here, but by drawing on a few of these writings I hope to clarify how I am using the word "value" and what it might mean for values to be *public*.

Readers may have noticed that the word "value" can be used in several different ways. In a first usage, values are properties of a subject—standards used repeatedly to make judgments and guide action. Used in this way, the word might refer to a feature of an individual person's character (as in the phrase "a person of strong moral values") or to something common to members of a group and embedded in various facets of their shared culture (as when a politician claims to represent "family values" or, say, "Indiana values"). In a second usage, values are properties of an object, as one might speak of a house, or a work of art, or a scholarly book as having value or values—monetary, ethical, aesthetic, and otherwise. For Dewey, primacy is given to a third usage: value as a verb, an active and ongoing process. It is through this process that values have their being. Personal values are constituted in acts and experiences of prizing and appraising and in patterns and habits of such valuing. Likewise, objects like "diamonds or mines and forests, are valuable when they are the objects of certain human activities" that give or assign them value (Dewey, 1939, p. 4). Such human activities are not limited to discrete acts of explicit evaluation but encompass any actions and experiences that involve tacit evaluations—for example, actions taken in order to create or attain value. These various senses of value are mutually dependent. To finally separate the subjective and objective meanings, says Dewey, would be like "attempt[ing] to solve a problem by riding two horses going in opposite directions" (1939, p. 5). This does not mean that we must restrict ourselves to one usage or the other, but that when the word is used in one way, the others are implied. If a student is said to develop certain values, this also amounts to and takes place through a change in worldly, value-laden actions and experiences.

Thus, the process of value development can be regarded as public in the following sense: Valuations take place in and through actions in a shared culture and are thus publicly accessible. A person's existing values have come about through interaction with an existing cultural background, and each new evaluation or value-laden action brings about some change in social reality. If no observable evidence of a value exists, says Dewey, then it makes no sense to speak of and is of no educational concern (1939). If valuing and value-directed learning are matters of action rather than acquisition, then they are to be judged not by what one internalizes but by what one does in a common cultural space that forms and sustains others. As we have already seen, the point is for students' learning to be judged not in terms of "what they are able to take in" but in what they "contribute to the common stock" (Dewey, 1903, p. 16).

Values can be described as public in a second, still stronger way. The word "public" suggests some relationship to a large group of people—those sharing a common concern or even the people as a whole (as in "the film-going public," "the general public," or "the public interest"). As laid out by Dewey in *The Public and Its Problems* (1927), a public forms when a group of disparate citizens comes together around some problem of mutual concern that lies outside of their control. For example, pollution from a factory might seep into the water used by various people who have no say in the factory's operations and who do not think of themselves as a group. By communicating with each other, they can work to solve the problem, perhaps by staging a boycott or by lobbying the state for regulatory intervention. Through this discourse, they become more aware of themselves as sharing common interests and, with time, more aware of themselves as a community.

Along these lines, during the process of assessing the projects created by CHP students regarding the Marion lynching, I asked for evaluations, positive or negative, from a variety of interested parties including librarians, historians, a newspaper editor, a prosecuting attorney, and other local citizens. I prompted interviewees to speak about what values the projects might have, both to the creators and to others. This framing allowed for a wide range of evaluations, but more than in most educational assessments, it encouraged people to consider consequences that lay outside the student and that thus impinged upon matters of shared interest. The interviews were conducted individually, but when discussing them in chapters to come, I place quotations into a sort of conversation with each other. If, in future projects, students and citizens were invited to participate in reading, learning, and discussing at a public event (much like a science fair or National History Day, with perhaps a stronger emphasis on contribution), they might begin to discover common interests in history, social justice, or the public schools. Their communication might, in turn, lay the groundwork for future learning and civic action.

Conclusion

In this chapter, I have reviewed a number of curricular programs that share the common feature of addressing learning that occurs through the creation of public products. These programs help to show that products and productive activities can fulfill a number of different roles in the learning process: They can be regarded as visible representations of students' skills or understandings, accessible for review by anyone seeking to assess student competence. Externalized, they are subject to revision and manipulation that can help students reach new understandings. As enactments, they present learning not as inert but as embedded in authentic tasks. Beyond all of that, they can create many different sorts of value for readers and others outside the school. In current educational practice, this final function strikes me as least well appreciated—and the values realized in this way as the least likely to be counted as real learning outcomes.

This blind spot has important implications. If productive work is taken to have consequences outside the school, then students have greater reason to pursue it passionately and greater responsibility to pursue it thoughtfully—to consider how each decision could make the work more or less valuable and in what ways. For students studying the Marion lynching, as described in this book, deciding how to produce well would involve considering both the reactions of prospective readers and important features of the historical and social context. (Historical narratives relating to lynching, race, and gender, for example, would inform one's understanding of what stories should be retold, and how.) While attempting to create products of value, students might also be led to consider how the books they are reading, the photos they are viewing, the videos they were watching, and the skills they are learning were themselves created to advance someone's purposes and values. In light of that, students would be faced with the need to read critically and decide which authors to trust and which sources to cite—what knowledge to build on and what to challenge. With these ideas in mind, I turn, in the following chapters, to Marion and the CHP, seeking to assess whether, in the field of history, this pedagogical approach can provide students with adequate or even exemplary opportunities to do work that they find interesting and consequential. By asking students and other citizens to reflect, broadly, on the values realized through students' productive work, I hope to draw attention to learning's status as a public phenomenon suffused with social and ethical implications.

· 3 ·

HISTORY IN THE ACT

I arrived in Marion in the closing days of March 2011 and was immediately surrounded by people and places from an earlier stage of my life. I unpacked a suitcase into my childhood bedroom and soon found myself walking the halls of Marion High School, from which I had graduated twelve years earlier. In this chapter, I explain how the project unfolded over two months in the spring of 2011, providing evidence of the project's scope, the time allotted, and the activities and teaching that took place. I also explain the sorts of data collection that I undertook, clarifying my role in the project as both a participant and an observer and providing context necessary to understand later chapters, which examine the nature and degree of value that this work had for students and members of the public. This narrative is far from a "how-to" manual, but I hope to provide some practical sense of how a project like this can be carried out.

Over the course of this description, it will become clear that the classroom differed from the norm in important ways, not least among them the fact that Mr. Munn and I—two adults—were both present. At the same time, however, the research site was a real classroom in an ordinary public high school. I aim to present a balanced analysis of the project and to reflect on what lessons are to be drawn from this research, so that readers might be in a position to consider whether this sort of project would be feasible in other classrooms.

My judgment is that under more typical circumstances, such a project would need to be less complicated, or be given more class time, or both—but that this would be time well spent.

Preparations

Soon after my return to Marion, I visited the two eleventh-grade U.S. history classes in which I was to work, introducing myself to the students as a researcher and a former student of Mr. Munn's. When the CHP was begun in the 1990s, projects were carried out mostly in Munn's Advanced Placement U.S. history classes. In the past several years, however, Marion High School had become part of the Advance College Program (ACP), offering classes through which students could earn Indiana University credit. Munn continued to teach one AP class, which focused on content from the AP syllabus and did not require any local history research. He also taught three ACP classes, which were somewhat more conceptually oriented. They included local history research and reached a broader slice of students—roughly a third of the graduating class, drawn from moderate to high levels of academic achievement. My research was conducted in the two largest ACP classes, which between them had approximately sixty students. The school as a whole enrolled about 1,350 ("School Snapshot, Marion High School," 2011).

In my introduction, I asked the students to call me by my first name and proceeded to explain the project and my research. Students would have a choice between three projects, I told them, and Munn had said as much before. In one option, they would study and create a wiki page on some aspect of the lynching that had taken place in Marion, with precise topics to be worked out later. Anyone choosing that option would take part in my study and would participate in interviews at the beginning and end of the project. Alternatively, students could participate in one of two interview projects, speaking either with a local veteran (a tried-and-true CHP assignment) or a Marion High School alumnus from before 1990 (a new experiment). Students choosing either of the latter two options would not be research subjects. In one class, eight students volunteered to participate in the study; in the other, eleven. Of these nineteen students—nine boys and ten girls—two identified as African American and fourteen as white. One was Latina, two others were Latino/a and white, and one identified as Chinese and white. Significantly, one of the students was also Munn's son. I call him Alex and interpret his project in light of the family relationship. He and I had not previously met, nor was I acquainted with any of the other students.[1]

The project played out over the course of the last eight weeks of the school year, with Thursday set aside as "project day." Some weeks, around the middle of the span, we spent only part of a class period on the project. As the end of school neared, we devoted more time, with students finalizing their wiki pages and presenting their work to the class. On project days, I participated actively, often providing feedback or facilitating discussion, while also taking notes, making audio recordings, and collecting relevant handouts. As the project developed, I came to spend more time working with the research subjects, with Munn overseeing but spending the bulk of his class time with the students working on other projects. This leads me to characterize my role as something like that of an apprentice teacher. Shortly after the classes, during free periods, I made further notes and added personal reflections. When project days kept me too engaged to observe fully, I attended and took notes on the instruction in a third ACP class, where students were also carrying out local history projects. In addition to Thursdays, I attended class several days each week, checking in with students and informally interviewing them about issues that arose in their work. Often, I stayed until Munn's end-of-day prep period, during which time we talked about the project's progress, planned future sessions, and discussed the history of the CHP. This chapter draws primarily on my field notes, supplemented by interviews with the students and Munn.

Given my standing relationship with Munn and my history of working with students on WikiMarion and the CHP, it would have been difficult for me to observe the project without participating in and thereby changing it. Rather than try, I chose to participate forthrightly and to push the project into a topic that Munn had not been able to undertake alone. By enacting the pedagogy, I was able to experience it from something like a teacher's perspective and to discuss it with Munn with a greater degree of understanding. As I have also noted, my participation allowed us to address a gap on the existing website and to study what I have called an extreme case that, I hoped, would reveal important features of this sort of learning. My active participation in the class has a number of implications, both for the success of the student projects and for the analysis and conclusions I present here and throughout this book. I was a guest in Munn's classroom and went there, in part, to learn about his practice. I did not assign grades or have any power to enforce discipline and, as mentioned, students generally called me by my first name. Still, I came from a prestigious university, took on a number of teacher-like tasks and carried something of a teacher's authority. I undoubtedly changed the situation by being there, providing a second adult presence and bringing my own set of knowledge and skills. I suspect that my presence also lent the project a feeling of greater importance.

To better understand the kind of history class students had experienced, I observed some of Munn's lessons outside the project. He had been my teacher during the mid-1990s, near the middle of his career. When I returned for this research, he was in his forty-second year of teaching, and the previous fall he had announced that it would be his last. Certain features remained the same as when I was a high schooler. Munn has a distinctive personal style, animated and enthusiastic, with a self-assured, avuncular eccentricity that he amplifies considerably in front of a room of students. In 2011, as before, he was known to burst into the classroom suddenly, exclaiming, "Scholars!" arms outstretched, before wisecracking with a student or two. Some would return his banter, playfully but usually with tongue in cheek. Others groaned. Over his desk hung a poster made for him by students—a parody of Shepherd Fairey's iconic "Hope" poster from Barack Obama's 2008 presidential campaign. In place of Obama's face was a picture of Mr. Munn, digitally stylized into a red, white, and blue stencil. Below it, in place of the word HOPE, the poster read, SCHOLARS.

The classroom was generally an intellectually lively place, rich with historical content. On days not devoted to project work, the class proceeded through twentieth-century history—the Progressive Era, the Great Depression, and the two world wars. Textbook reading was assigned regularly from the widely used, upper-level textbook *The American Pageant* and class time was often spent doing close reading of supplementary sources—primary and secondary—or watching a clip from a historical documentary (Bailey, Kennedy, & Cohen, 2001). I saw occasional instances of group work and opportunities for class presentation. In one, students were divided into groups and assigned to research different factors contributing to the outbreak of World War I. The following day, they created PowerPoint presentations and delivered them to the class. As for technology, two computers sat at Munn's desk: a Mac and an older PC. One was connected to an LCD projector. Next door was a large computer lab, which could be reserved in advance but often had free terminals where a few of our students could work. The class also used Moodle—a private course website with calendar, online grade book, and electronic submission of some assignments.

Local history also played an important role in the classroom, of course. Munn's knowledge of the community clearly gave him an understanding of his students and their families, enabling a sort of historically inflected form of what is sometimes called "culturally responsive teaching" (Ladson-Billings, 1995). I have already described a particularly striking lesson revolving around Lewis Hine's photographs of a Marion glass factory, and at other times it was clear that Munn's knowledge of the community informed his knowledge of students. There were also occasions when he carried on about local history, digressively, in ways that seemed to strain student attention spans. During my opening interviews, in an effort to gauge students' background knowledge, I asked what, if anything, they had heard people say about the lynching. One reported hearing, from Munn's previous students, that "talking about the lynching is a good way to get him off subject." (Besides this, numerous students reported that what little they had heard of the lynching came from Mr. Munn's passing comments. Midway through my time in the class, when the course reached the 1920s and 1930s, he covered it with the whole class, showing his favorite of the documentaries [Gould, 1998], leading a discussion and assigning a written reflection).

Introductory interviews

In my first week in the classroom, which I am not counting among the eight weeks of the project, I conducted introductory interviews with the students. These were intended to help acquaint me with the students and to elicit their feelings about history and history class, their knowledge of the lynching, and their feelings about race in Marion.[2] In a few cases, they allowed me to compare student thinking at the beginning and end of a project. Most significantly, though, they provided a chance to meet the students, establish a relationship, and get to know their interests—a knowledge that proved helpful in formulating paper topics. A student I call David told me that he was interested in law and spoke of having a strong sense of justice. Ashley, I learned, was highly involved in her church. When I asked students about their career plans, most casually listed a few general possibilities. Ashley told me, with startling certitude, that she had been "called to be a missionary." Nick informed me that he was interested in doing some kind of project related to mapping. All of these comments eventually factored into their project choices.

The Gospel According to James

A month before my return to Indiana, I learned that about the time the project was set to begin, a stage play based on the Marion lynching would be debuting at the Indiana Repertory Theater in Indianapolis. The play, *The Gospel According to James*, was inspired by James Madison's book and a playwright at Ohio University had been commissioned to write it. It was to be in Indianapolis for only three weeks before moving to Chicago, and, surprisingly to me, it was not widely discussed in Marion. The play was briefly announced in the *Chronicle-Tribune* only five days before the end of its run and was featured in a not-quite four-hundred-word article with two days remaining ("Indy Stage Hosting Play With Marion Ties," 2011, "Play Chronicles Marion History," 2011). One morning during my first week back, I attended a matinee intended for school audiences. The house, however, was mostly empty. A number of my research subjects would see a later performance.

The central conceit of the play is a fictionalized 1980s meeting between Mary Ball, back in Marion for the funeral of her father, and James Cameron, who has also returned to town, documentary camera crew in tow, to receive a pardon from the governor. On a sparsely set stage, the two tell rival versions of the story, about which Cameron is eager to talk but which Ball had spent her life trying to escape. As the two survivors speak, the events they describe are acted out in front of them, with a focus on their differing memories of the shooting, the alleged rape, and the relationships among the characters. The lynching itself is not enacted on stage but is represented in a stylized way using sound and shadow.

The character "James" relates much the same story that his real-life counterpart told publicly from the 1980s onward. In this version, Cameron, a naïve shoe-shine boy, reluctantly accompanied the older Shipp and Smith on an attempted robbery. Handed a gun, however, and realizing that the target, Claude Deeter, was a customer and friend, he fled the scene, hearing gunshots behind him. In the play, the 1980s Mary, who goes by "Marie," questions this story and suggests that he might be protecting his own reputation and profiting from his newfound fame. In one pitched exchange, Ball implores Cameron to tell the truth. "I am telling the truth," he replies, "the gospel truth." She fires back, sarcastically, "Yeah, the gospel according to James" (Smith, 2011). This title line, with its biblical allusion, conveys at least two important features of the play. First, it presents the lynching as an event weighty with an almost-sacred significance. Second, it captures the way in which the events are known only through the accounts of witnesses—some of them, like Cameron's, recorded decades later—that often conflict and are colored by the views and interests of whoever is doing the talking. The real Mary Ball left no version of the story, but as the play progresses, Marie offers one, drawn largely from tales that have circulated around Marion. In this hazy version of events, the five principal players formed a stickup gang, the young Mary and Abram Smith were lovers, and the shooting was the result of squabbling within the group. By the end of the play, this story, too, is problematized, leaving audience members to make sense of contending, mutually contradictory memories.

A field trip to see the play was out of the question. With the school in its fourth year of academic probation for low test scores, and with an interim principal in charge, no new trips were being approved. Instead, we encouraged students working on the project to attend a weekend show. Attendance did not factor into the students' grades, but I offered to pay, from research funds, the cost of a student-rate ticket for any student who wanted to attend, along with a parent ticket, if necessary. Six of the nineteen went—Carmen and Hannah together, Jennifer with her mother, and Julia, Tom, and Alex in a car with Bill Munn and his wife.[3] On the way back into town, Munn's group stopped at a few of the lynching sites. Julia and Alex began to conceive of some kind of memorial or event, and Tom learned that the site of the original shooting was located mere blocks from his house. For some of the students, the play seemed to have its intended effect. I spoke with four of them, in a group, a few days afterward, and all were impressed by its weight. Hannah began by saying she "had a lot more questions after seeing it than before seeing it," and Carmen agreed. This was helpful in some ways. It helped Hannah, for one, realize that "no one knew for sure… about what exactly happened" and to appreciate the number of "different perspectives" available. But it also led to some confusion about which events were factual and which were fictional. When I informally polled them about the veracity of certain plot points, there was little consensus.

Weeks one through three: Background and topic selection

I had managed to conduct introductory interviews with these six students before they saw the play, but I spent the early part of the following week finishing my talks with the rest of their classmates. That Thursday, April 13, the lynching project began in earnest. (For a week-by-week schedule, see

Table 1.) Munn and I had discussed the day's lesson in advance and decided that he would speak to students working on interviews while I talked with those studying the lynching. I describe here some of his instruction to the students working on other projects, based on our planning session and my observations in the third class, because it suggests the accumulated wisdom we were drawing on. It also reveals some principles that apply in the lynching project—the interviews conducted by several participants, but also the other projects in a more general way. To these students, who had already begun to identify subjects for their oral history interviews, Mr. Munn distributed consent forms and a project checklist. His main focus of instruction, though, was on a questionnaire that would help students begin to plan for their interviews. To complete it, they would need to talk with their subjects once before the actual interview. This would help them determine what their interviewees had to say—or whether they were ready to talk at all. Some veterans like to reminisce about their war buddies, Munn explained, whereas others haven't yet processed their experiences. In future weeks, with this information in hand, students would begin to formulate questions.

Table 1: Project Schedule.

	Week Beginning	Main Activities
Preparation	04/04/11	Preliminary interviews with students begin. Some students see play.
Week 1	04/11/11	Preliminary interviews conclude. Students do background reading.
Week 2	04/18/11	Students discuss background reading and take stock of available resources. Most students select project topics.
Week 3	04/25/11	Students submit project proposals, finalizing topics. As a group, we set a work schedule.
Week 4	05/02/11	Students attend orientation sessions at the public library's local history room and begin collecting data.
Week 5	05/09/11	Students outline papers. I provide wiki-editing tutorial. Mr. Munn begins emphasizing deadlines.
Week 6	05/16/11	Drafts are due. Students write and help one another with writing and wiki editing.
Week 7	05/23/11	Drafts are edited. Some students finish projects. Presentations begin.

Week 8	05/30/11	Students finish wiki pages and presentations. School year ends. Final interviews with students begin.
Later		Final interviews conclude. Mr. Munn and I are contacted by some readers of the site. I attempt to follow up with some students.

When Munn taught the lesson, he offered a rule of thumb for question writing: "If people in 2050 found a book of interviews, what would they want to know about?"[4] Not only did he ask students to consider their audience, then, but he also encouraged them to think about their projects as having potential value over a time frame of multiple generations. This long-term perspective is reflected in some of the student comments I report in Chapter 4, and it serves as a reminder, even as I report on the reactions of present-day readers in Chapter 5, that the audience and future uses for the work are always partially indeterminate. His lesson design and pieces of advice were built on past experience, Munn told me. He had seen projects rendered unusable by the absence of consent forms, and he knew that the preparatory questionnaires would improve the quality of the eventual interviews. The prewriting tasks would break a large project down into manageable stages, limiting procrastination. Still, he explained in a later conversation, these deadlines were best treated flexibly, because students' work progress could be delayed by their interviewees' schedules or by technical difficulties.

Many of the same principles applied to the lynching project—scaffolded planning stages, frequent but flexible deadlines, and consideration of a public audience. The immediate needs of the lynching project, though, were somewhat different. First, students needed topics and, to select these, a bit of background knowledge. Munn and I decided that I would show students some of the most important books on the lynching. By this point, most had already seen Madison's book or even begun to read it, and I also introduced the books by James Cameron and Cynthia Carr, provided context on each, and led a short discussion on the possible merits and limitations that each might have as historical sources. I asked all students to read the first six pages from Madison's book—a retelling of the basic events—and then allowed them to divide up other chapters, which they were to read and summarize for the group in a written paragraph. This, Munn and I thought, would help them develop knowledge of the event, take stock of what had been written, contribute to the group effort, and begin to consider what products would be interesting and valuable.

Upon my arrival the following day, Munn directed me to one corner of the classroom, where two students, whom I will call X and Y, had been arguing. I moved to investigate, but X approached me first, saying, "Rob, I have something to ask you. Do you think the lynching was civil justice or racism?" X had argued for "civil justice," Y for racism. I was taken aback. This called to mind an idea common in white Marion—that although its vigilantism was unfortunate, the fact that the mob spared Cameron shows it to have been essentially just. In a nod to this notion, Madison's book includes a chapter called "A Fair Mob," a phrase taken from the Court of Inquiry testimony of a Marion police captain (Madison, 2001, chap. 6). Relatedly, I have heard modern-day Marionites claim that lynching was somehow less of an atrocity, and unworthy of continuing attention, because it resulted in the deaths of two killers (never mind that it is entirely unclear who was responsible for Claude Deeter's shooting). X did not sound like an apologist, exactly—or if that was the effect of the words, then the genial spirit in which they were offered seemed to call for at least a temporary suspension of judgment. As we talked, X did acknowledge the racial dimension and stated the position in a way that calls to mind a kind of intellectual contrarianism. I paraphrased X's statement in my notes: "Everyone else says it was racism, but I wanted to argue that it was also civil justice." If it were *only* racism, X argued, why would the mob have stopped before Cameron, or the other black inmates? If it were civil justice, Y countered, citing a page in Madison's book, why had the mob spared other criminals in the jail?[5]

The exchange was perplexing, not only because it jarred my moral sensibilities, but also because the terms from which the debate began—the labels the students sought to apply—were such simple binaries. In retrospect, this seems to have been an initial attempt to make sense of a troubling event, in which both students quickly took stands and defended them. We briefly revisited the issue the following Thursday, but after that, attention turned to the creation of wiki pages, and this thread of conversation was dropped. In our final interview, as an afterthought, I asked X about this issue again. X's position may have softened somewhat; there were now three factors at play: racism, civil justice, and mob mentality. But the position remained substantially the same, and the spirit was every bit as good natured as before. I remain troubled that in the rush to publish, this product-directed work—or my implementation of it—provided insufficient opportunity initially to work through important issues.

At this point in the project, a few students had moved toward topic selection, but most had not. Over the years, project ideas have come from both student proposals and Mr. Munn's suggestions, which are sometimes just the kernel of an idea and other times a document or a lead for a student to pursue. Having learned that Tom lived near the scene of the shooting, the road once called Lovers' Lane, Munn pointed him to a vertical file in the Indiana Room that contained interesting newspaper clippings about criminal activity in the surrounding neighborhood, then known by the mysterious name "Dark Secret." Another student expressed a desire to interview his grandmother, and Munn encouraged him, knowing her to be an oral historian of African American experiences in Marion. I, too, found myself uncovering a number of research possibilities—or rather, they were brought to me. My mother, a speech therapist in the school district, had mentioned the project to others in her school's office and was told of a ninety-year-old woman who remembered living in Marion during the lynching and could speak about it lucidly. Later, my mother ran into a retired school administrator named Carol Secttor, who claimed to have received a threatening note from the Klan as a young teacher in the early 1970s. In this sort of interaction, I began to appreciate what it was like to be a teacher enmeshed in these networks of local history and memory—learning what was important to people, what resources were available, and how a value-producing school might serve its community.

Not all of the research leads were related to the lynching. My sister informed me that the school's illustrious "show choir" was being credited with inventing the form, having added choreography to a traditional "swing choir" routine at a competition in 1974, but the sources were not entirely reputable (Show Choir Canada, 2010). Fox's television series about show choir, *Glee*, was then popular among high schoolers, and some of the students were children of former members of the group, making the topic seem promising for future study. As I have said, the overriding theme of the CHP has been race, but a topic like *Glee* and show choir suggests the range of other themes that might be available. In this case, the arts are at issue, with possible notes of gender and sexual orientation, but one can imagine projects on class, technology, religion, and many other themes.

Back at school, planning for week two, Munn and I developed a list of potential research topics. As I have said, some students, including Jason, Alex, Zachary, and Julia, had already begun to formulate ideas on their own. Others, such as Tom, Caleb, Hannah, and Carmen, had latched onto early or offhand suggestions and begun to pursue them. In still other cases, we had projects in mind for certain students, and they found the ideas appealing. Munn feared that one sensitive student might be best suited to a project that addressed the lynching indirectly. With a few musically inclined students, I floated the idea of a project on the song "Strange Fruit." But for the remaining students who had yet to settle on a topic, we drew up a list—biographies, specific events, locations, and important contextual features. Munn, like my mother, knew Carol Secttor and had heard her story. He even seemed to recall that it bore some relation to the lynching. We added it to the list. That Thursday, I put these possibilities in front of the students, and they asked questions and began to claim topics. Most seemed to leave satisfied; a few others continued to negotiate and brainstorm into the next week. (A list of student projects is provided in Table 2.)

Table 2: Student Project Topics.

	Pseudonym	Project Topic
Period 2	Nick	Map of sites relating to the lynching
	Alexis	The Beitler lynching photograph
	Tom	Lovers' Lane; also worked on home page
	Caleb	1970s letter to teacher from Ku Klux Klan; also worked on home page
	Lynn	Newspaper coverage of the lynching
	Samantha	The song "Strange Fruit"
	David	Legal response to the lynching
	Ben	Sheriff Jake Campbell (originally Marion Police)
Period 5	Jennifer	The Roaring Twenties in Marion—local context
	Michael	Thomas Shipp, lynching victim
	Hannah	*The Gospel According to James*
	Alex	Lynching memorialization and reconciliation
	Julia	Lynching in national context
	Carmen	*The Gospel According to James*
	Emily	Mary Ball, alleged rape victim and accuser of Thomas Shipp and Abram Smith
	Eric	Guide to resources about the lynching
	Zachary	Organizations that may have contributed to the lynching
	Ashley	The role of churches in the lynching and response
	Jason	Interview with grandmother

On the workday during the third week of the project, students shared what they had learned from their distributed reading assignments. They then hand-wrote project proposals that formalized their topic choices—a common step in projects through the years. We closed by sketching out a timetable for the next month: Before May 5, locate your sources and begin taking notes. By May 12, research should be drawing to a close, with writing begun. By May 19, drafts should be in place so that class time could be spent editing. By May 26, students should be proofreading and putting on finishing touches. This was arrived at mostly through group discussion among the students, though I encouraged them to move the milestones up slightly. Looking back, this week seems relatively uneventful, when compared with the hectic closing stretch, and given the chance to repeat the work, I would be inclined to consolidate these activities and set the milestones even earlier.

Weeks four and five: Research and early writing

With topics more or less settled, week four brought the project into a research phase. I have already mentioned, while describing the life of the CHP, that the Marion Public Library has long been a key partner. As this section of our work approached, Munn notified the director of the Indiana Room, the library's local history collection, that we needed to schedule orientation sessions as had been done in the past. I stopped by to check on resources and arrange times. The most important physical resource I found was a collection of binders, in which the Indiana Room's resident lynching expert, a staff member named Betty Reynolds, had compiled hundreds or perhaps thousands of documents on the lynching, ranging from the immediate aftermath to the more recent explosion of interest. The majority of the resources were articles from Marion's newspapers, but they also included legal depositions and articles from across the region and nation. Betty's prior work and her presence during the project were significant assets. The library also had copies of the books mentioned above and other resources: a sourcebook on lynching and a series of older works as well as digitized copies of television documentaries and *Without Sanctuary*, a harrowing collection of lynching photography (Allen, 2000).

The library staff helpfully consolidated most of the relevant books and binders into a single bookcase, and Betty led several orientation sessions in which she introduced students to the resources and basic guidelines for using the room. After hearing their topics, she provided personalized help, showing students vertical files, digital census records, death certificates, city directories, and other library collections. When Betty was unavailable, other staff members provided basic orientation, and I repeated some of the guidance I had heard her give. Before the project, few, if any, of the students had ever visited the Indiana Room. For some, it was also a first encounter with the politics of lynching memory. In the course of explaining how she had come to compile the resources, Betty mentioned that a previous library supervisor had forbidden any work on the lynching. I recorded in my notes that one student looked "confused" and "slightly slack-jawed" at this suggestion. A different student—X from the earlier argument, who argued for "civil justice"—when scrolling through the library's digitized collection of historical photographs and finding no copy of the infamous Beitler image, exclaimed, "They're trying to cover this up!" Betty, an active but older woman, also provided students with a link to the past. She often spoke of her grandfather, who had been pressured to join the Klan. When he refused, she said, he was fired from a job and had his best horse poisoned. She was quick to point out, though, that the Klan was a broad social organization with an agenda and activities that went beyond racism. This sort of storytelling, along with Betty's obvious investment in Marion's past, provided a sense of the public importance of lynching history and of how the event had been remembered and suppressed through the years. In this, it also speaks to the sort of community members that educators and students can enlist in this sort of work.

Between the library's irregular hours and students' spring sports schedules and other commitments, finding time for these sessions was a challenge. Eventually, we were able to set a few meeting days that, between them, worked for most students. I attended these and, whenever possible, was also present for later sessions when students returned to work on their own time. My attendance was made necessary by my research role, and I attempted to back off and let the students explore on their own, but of course there were times when I helped. This was a clear case where my availability made feasible a portion of the research that would otherwise have been more onerous.

Having made a point of flexible deadlines early in the project, by the fifth week Mr. Munn conveyed a sense of greater urgency to the class. "There are no excuses now," he announced, telling students doing interview projects that their transcripts were due the following week and those researching the lynching that their drafts should be complete by then. He also provided transcription tips and encouragement: Write down all of your questions first, and then fill in the responses. Take it a few at a time. "It goes slowly at first. But then you really get going." Presentations for the interview projects would begin on May 20, and he would take volunteers first. Lynching presentations would come last, giving the students time to finish their wiki pages.

I then took the students aside for another work session. Munn had selected a rubric for the lynching project based on one produced by National History Day, which he had used with the students in the past. It included elements such as historical accuracy, context, analysis, use of available sources, demonstration of significance, and clarity of presentation. I distributed it and answered a few questions about how the rubric applied or did not apply to individual projects. Ultimately, the rubric played a relatively minor role in this work for both teacher and students, with less attention given to satisfying its individual points and more to satisfying the audience and doing justice to the historical event. Rubrics have value in providing structure and clear expectations to a class, but it strikes me as healthy to focus students' attention on the ultimate goals as much as possible, in order to prevent the activity from becoming an exercise in checking off boxes. I would recommend a relatively simple rubric, with each point clearly tied to an overarching goal of creating value—citation linked to convincing an audience, narrative linked to holding its attention, etc.

For the rest of that period, events in the morning and afternoon classes diverged. In one class, Caleb had just finished his interview with Carol Secttor. She had kept her letter from the KKK along with its envelope and an assortment of Klan propaganda materials, some of which had handwritten notes scrawled atop. Caleb had brought the materials to class, and we passed them around the group, sharing in the excitement of his discovery. In the other class, students had time to outline. During this work session, many of them came to me with questions. A few wanted feedback on their outlines—Did this thesis statement look okay? Where could they find evidence for a certain point? Ashley, researching church involvement in the 2003 reconciliation events, was having trouble understanding which pastors she needed to talk to. I referred her to Munn's son Alex, who, by that point, knew more about the subject than I did. Alex, in turn, was waiting on a response to an email he had sent Cynthia Carr. "I've been assuming I will get one," he said, but Hannah, overhearing the conversation, interrupted, "Don't assume that." She had been hoping to interview a cast member from *The Gospel According to James,* but her emails had gone unanswered, and the prospects were looking dim. I was pleased to see students developing knowledge and practical research experience and then sharing it with each other.

At first, this required my assistance—probably because of my greater knowledge of the event and website, and because, from my vantage point, I could better see the intersections between their projects. But increasingly, as students' knowledge developed, they found these opportunities on their own. Many students inserted links between their projects and helped each other with technical aspects of wiki creation. Several, especially Tom, formulated creative plans to link the projects to each other and organize them into a whole. While working at the public library, I observed Emily, Julia, and Ashley comparing and sharing information they had found. In our final interview, Ashley mentioned this scene, of "going through and helping [Julia] and [Emily] and different people—looking at their stuff. I learned a lot about all the other factors, like with Mary Ball, and realizing how complicated it was." She went on to explain, "Afterward, we were just all interested in each other's parts and what they were finding, because it was, again, just part of the mystery of researching all that. So, we were talking about that more at school... about... what we found, because it was kind of an exciting thing for us." This sort of mutual interest and assistance did not reach full flower, but it might be encouraged by allowing more time for students to share progress reports or pose questions to the group.

Finally, with the writing stage of the project fast approaching, I showed students how to create and edit wiki pages. Unlike a modern word processing program, in which the user can highlight a word, apply formatting, and then view the word as it will appear in print, our wiki software requires the user to know a set of codes—combinations of keyboard characters that allow the user to create headings, insert images, add italics, and perform other formatting tasks. Standardized testing led to unplanned changes in the schedule, giving us unexpected extra time in one class that allowed me to give a tutorial.

In the other class, testing took time away—just one of the many distractions that seemed to multiply as the year's end approached. Periods were repeatedly interrupted by earthquake drills and tornado warnings. Observers came from the ACP program and a state turnaround team, and one daylong physics field trip to an amusement park—registered, apparently, before the ban was instituted—left the class half full. Working around these interruptions, I pulled students aside in small groups, checked on their progress, and demonstrated the basic skills of wiki editing. Many of the students picked these up very quickly, and the best were able to help peers who struggled or had received limited demonstrations of the wiki. For more advanced formatting, they were able to copy elements from existing wiki pages.

Weeks six through eight: Editing and presentation

On May 19—week six of the project, with two remaining—the students were to have completed drafts. The day was scheduled for "peer editing," but there was still such a wide variety among projects in terms of format and progress made that I simply encouraged students to work on whatever aspect of their project was most pressing. Some did pair off and read each other's drafts, but did not follow any formal protocol. Some needed help with wiki formatting, and fortunately other students were usually able to provide it. One had handwritten his text but needed time alone to type. Another was still finishing the draft. This flexibility was probably made possible by students' prior instruction in group work and their general cooperativeness, but again, I did find it preferable—and probably necessary, in order to finish on time—simply to let students do what needed to be done.

To that point, I had avoided editing any student wiki pages, but Nick ran into trouble formatting his map—a technically demanding task. After he had exhausted all of the solutions he could think of, I broke down and found one myself. Some students needed help with their writing or wiki formatting, while others were on track to finish early and had demonstrated a good eye for writing. I asked some of them to work together, making an effort to pair students with complementary skills. For others, I marked up drafts and returned them. Earlier in this chapter, I noted that the third week of the project seemed slow and marginally useful. By the seventh week, from my position, the work started to feel more frantic. I had forgotten how in the final days of school distractions multiply and, with testing over and summer near, even motivated students lose attention. This part of the project would have benefited from more time, under circumstances more conducive to thoughtful revision.

As the final days of school approached, presentations began. Students working on the veterans' and school history projects went first, while those working on lynching projects were in the computer lab next door, putting finishing touches on their wiki pages. In the last three days of school, students on the lynching project gave their class presentations. Considering the fact that the students were pressed for time, Munn allowed them to be relatively informal. Rather than developing PowerPoint presentations, they simply projected their finished web pages in front of the class and spoke—some extemporaneously and others from notes. I spent some of this time out of the room, conducting final interviews. Thus, I witnessed some but not all of these presentations.

The final interviews, which are examined at length in Chapter 4, reveal some of the remarkable ways in which students thought about their work. But in other ways, the project's final days strike me as having been anticlimactic. The work was rushed, most students' minds were on summer vacation, and even at the end, the wiki cover page was only half finished. (Munn and I later filled in the gaps, a fact of which I informed the outside readers interviewed for Chapter 5.) Perhaps this is to be expected. Publication deadlines are often chaotic, and distractions and time pressures are endemic to the large public high school. Still, given the centrality of the public audience to this project, the moment of publication should be cause for celebration.

If anything, I should note, this project emphasized publication more than others had done in the past. In the projects on veterans' and school history, students gave more formal class presentations, but their projects were not posted—merely archived with the implication that some would be posted at a later date. For many years, students submitted their final papers in page protectors, which were assembled into binders in class, then later placed on file at the library. Some students have posted their own work to the web, but probably more often their submission was actually an act of archiving. Publication came later on, if ever. If publication motivates students' quality work and gives their learning a different character, it seems important to publish consistently, issue press releases, announce new work on a blog or in an email newsletter, and celebrate the occasion with a release party—perhaps with guests from outside the class, to add importance and so that students could observe audience reactions.

Aftermath of the Project

The project nominally came to a close in the first days of June, but several students had expressed interest in ongoing involvement, a few loose ends remained, and the public life of the work had just begun. When summer came, most of the students' intended extensions came to naught. Late in the project, for example, Emily learned of the existence of new evidence—a collection of audiotapes in a university archive in Indianapolis. She had been told, by Cynthia Carr, that the tapes included an interview with a nurse who had treated Mary Ball the night of the crime. Possessed by the thought that this recording might shed light on the rape allegations, she tried to find audio online or to have them sent via interlibrary loan to Indiana Wesleyan. Nothing panned out in time, but she was still hoping to make the trip before her family moved, cross-country, a few weeks into the summer. I attempted to contact her later that summer to see whether anything had become of the plans, but I received no response. Besides Emily, several students had expressed an intention to come back during the summer and finish the incomplete main page of the exhibit. Midway through the vacation, I sent emails asking whether they were still interested but, again, no response came. Some students had also talked about follow-up projects such as a "prayer walk" or a public forum. With the right infrastructure in place—a service-learning class the following autumn, or the extracurricular group that nurtured projects at Marion High School in the 1990s—something might have come of this. As it happened, though, I returned to California, Munn retired, and any remaining momentum was lost.

On a somewhat more positive note, Ashley had ended the year looking for a photograph of the plaque that, she read, had been approved by the county commissioners to be displayed in city hall. The plaques were down for renovation, complicating the task. She emailed me in early June about her ongoing efforts and followed up a few weeks later, saying:

> The guy who supposedly is in charge of the placement of the court house plaques and things didn't even know there was such a plaque. I had to back myself with evidence in the *Chronicle-Tribune* to make him believe me, and then he simply said he didn't know anything about it.

Despite the fact that Ashley reached what she called a "dead end," I was impressed by her persistence and resourceful use of evidence in taking civic action. Later that summer, I came across the source of the error. Ashley had found a 2003 article reporting that the Grant County commissioners approved the plaque on a vote of two to one. But this was not the end of the story—shortly thereafter, the *Chronicle-Tribune* ran another article headlined "Revote: No Plaque" (Harty, 2003). I emailed Ashley this discovery, and she promptly logged into her wiki page, corrected the error, and added a paragraph.

We did not announce the publication of the wiki pages, but people managed to find them anyway. Within two weeks of the end of school, Munn was contacted by an activist in Milwaukee. She was circulating a proposal for an online lynching museum, was impressed by the students' work, and wanted to speak more with their teacher. Four months later, in the fall of 2011, Munn was contacted by Loren Ghiglione, a journalism professor writing his own book while crossing the country with one of his Northwestern students and one recent alumnus. Ghiglione praised the WikiMarion exhibit, requested to meet with some students, and ended up having coffee with Julia, Alex, and Bill Munn one Sunday morning as the group passed through town.

Reflections and conclusion

One noteworthy feature of this type of work is the character of the relationship between student and teacher. Under more traditional arrangements—and through much of the year, in Mr. Munn's classroom—the teacher instructs or perhaps facilitates learning and then examines the student. In the sort of work I participated in, teacher and student are both engaged in an effort to learn things neither of them fully understands and to contribute to groups larger than both of them, whose judgments none can fully anticipate. If the project is successful, students come to know more about their topic of research than the teacher, which places the two on a somewhat more even plane than is usually the case. The relationship resembles what Soep and Chávez (2010) call "collegial pedagogy" in their study of Youth Radio, a nonprofit organization in which students learn to produce media by collaborating, outside of school, with skilled adult producers. Soep and Chávez define collegial pedagogy as "a relationship in which two or more people jointly engage in a significant task for shared purposes, with collective responsibility" (2010, p. 53). Certain features of this definition do not fit the research seen in Munn's classroom. Work there is sometimes collaborative, and teacher and students have some shared stake in the outcome, but as currently practiced, final responsibility is individual, not collective. The CHP takes place in a high school classroom, whereas Youth Radio is extracurricular, and the academic curriculum and thus the discipline of history have greater weight in its goals. Nevertheless, I would like to suggest that certain features common to the CHP and Youth Radio—such as an audience and purpose beyond the learning context—to some extent imply the less adversarial relationship that both cases share. I say this tentatively, acknowledging that my experience may also reflect my unique position in the class as neither student nor teacher.

From the description provided in this chapter, the picture that emerges is of a real classroom with real distractions and time pressures, and of work that resembles a more typical class project even as it varies the formula. It cannot be denied that we had certain advantages that enabled us to pursue a project more complicated than would be easily achievable under normal circumstances. Thus, the point is not that our results are generalizable, statistically speaking, in their current form. The project is best taken as a provocation and examination: a provocation to consider that students' work can do more than prove their own learning, and yet that one proof of learning—and proof that the learning has been worthwhile—lies in its value for others. It depicts a project that stretches the bounds of what is currently achievable in a classroom, but which is close enough that it could be brought within reach by further pedagogical and technological development. Here, I present a few reflections, based on my experience with the project, on how much of a challenge various obstacles present and how they could be made more feasible.

I have, by now, noted on several occasions that implementing the project in this form depended on having two adults present. Munn and I had designed the project to be comparable in scope to those done in other years, and he confirmed on multiple occasions that this was the case. I tend to think this is true of the students' individual projects—that is, their scope was similar to other projects done this year or in years past. This year, however, the range of student projects was unusually wide, meaning that more teacher attention was required. With students working on so many different kinds of projects—interviews, archival research, context setting, multimedia production—they needed a level of personalized instruction and feedback that a single teacher might struggle to provide.

While acknowledging this difficulty, the project could be made more feasible in several ways. Although it played out over a long period of time, relatively few class periods were taken up. One teacher could accomplish something similar by devoting more days to the project, either stretched out over a whole semester or massed in a four- or six-week unit. It would also be helpful if some of the writing and revision were handled in an English class. This strategy was employed in the early years of the CHP when Marion High School offered English and history classes in a coordinated humanities or American studies program. Finally, a teacher would do well to focus on one or two types of research at a time, as Munn typically does, offering students a choice between several topics and otherwise allowing limited exceptions to students with the demonstrated capacity to work independently.

For purposes of this study, the diversity of student products offers a significant benefit: It allowed me to examine, in a brief time, many different shades of historical learning. In Chapter 4, I discuss in more detail the individual projects and the wide range of educational values that students identified in their own work. This work, as we carried it out in 2011, resembles a standard class project in many of its basic stages and elements. (If anything, perhaps it should differ more, with explicit discussion of opportunities to create value, and then, at the end, encounters with an audience.) Work remains to be done before a project like this could be widely implemented. The following two chapters show why such an effort would be worthwhile.

· 4 ·

"PEOPLE NEED TO KNOW"

In previous chapters, I have provided a rationale for investigating learning that occurs as students contribute value to communities outside the school. I have also described the contexts in which I chose to study it—Marion, the CHP, and the particular students and classes who, in spring 2011, set out to create a set of articles and resources on the 1930 Marion lynching. This chapter and the next form the empirical heart of the book, reporting on the various forms of value created by these students' work. I first look at this value as perceived by the students themselves before turning, in Chapter 5, to public perceptions of the project.

The evidence here is drawn primarily from interviews conducted with each student at the project's end, contextualized using evidence from field notes, earlier interviews, and quotations taken directly from student web pages. The interviews included a variety of questions designed to elicit what sorts of value, if any, students saw in the project. They were asked, for example, about the experience of working on the project and about what, if any, value they saw in their work, followed by a range of more specific follow-up questions. (Full interview protocols and methodological details are provided in the Appendix.) Late in the interview, students were presented with term papers that they had written in the same class as a first-semester project. Those earlier papers, which covered topics in U.S. history prior to the Civil War, were similar to the wiki projects in scope, but they had been read and graded by Mr. Munn alone and were not written for any public audience. The students were then asked to compare the experiences of working on the two projects and the points of value they saw in each. (Note that this technique was used to prompt reflection on the uniquely public aspects of the wiki project, but it does not constitute a comparative research design.)

The chapter is organized into three main sections. The first addresses the distinguishing feature of the project—the opportunity it afforded students to create products for an audience outside the school—gauging the extent to which students found this a worthwhile goal and exploring the variety of specific values they identified. As I will show, nearly all students endorsed this aim, and many were able to articulate insightful reasons for their projects' value. In the second and third sections of the chapter, I trace other forms of thought and practice that the project called forth: first, in terms of the skills and knowledge of academic history; then, in a more personal sort of historical sense-making wherein students reflected on their communities and their own places in them. Taken as a whole, the evidence presented in this chapter indicates that students saw their projects as valuable public contributions and that through their work on these projects, they honed research skills, crafted texts, and constructed knowledge. Having accomplished all of this in the course of personally meaningful, value-creating activity, many of the students showed signs of appreciating the significance of historical learning in their own lives and in the life of their community.

Public value

With regard to personal growth and social commitment, one of the more compelling projects was carried out by Jason, the star athlete in Munn's class.[1] A former quarterback on the football team, Jason had been forced to give up the sport after a series of injuries. His baseball career continued, however, and the project took place during the high school baseball season, which he described as a "twenty-four seven job." In our opening interview, he told me that he dreamed someday of playing right field for the New York Yankees or, failing that, of becoming an architect. From the start of the project, Jason wanted to interview his grandmother, whom he knew to be interested in the lynching. He did not fully appreciate the nature or depth of her interest, but Munn did and encouraged him to go forward.

Jason's grandmother was a retired secretary and schoolteacher, and, it turned out, an oral historian of Marion's African American community. At an orientation session in the Indiana Room, he was awed to see the fruits of her research—a binder of transcripts and, sitting next to it on the library shelf, a self-published book that included interviews with, among others, great-grandparents Jason had never known. Having looked through her work and read James Madison's basic account of the lynching, Jason wrote questions for their interview. Munn had provided question-writing guidance in class—mostly for the benefit of students doing other projects, because the lynching project was less interview-centric. The day before the interview, I talked with Jason and helped him revise the questions, encouraging him to make them more open ended and to ask about topics that I suspected would address his grandmother's interests.[2] After conducting the interview, though, he reported that the questions had been mostly unnecessary; his grandmother spoke freely and covered most of the points without being asked. She explained the purpose behind her book, which she hoped would draw attention to a division among African Americans in Grant County—between the old, usually light-skinned families who settled in the town of Weaver in the mid-nineteenth century and the darker-skinned families, like her own, that migrated north in the early twentieth century. She then discussed the lynching itself, how she learned of it from her mother and father, and the stories of the event that circulated in different African American families.

The following week, Jason visited his grandmother's house each evening after baseball practice, and the two transcribed the interview. "It took forev-er," he told me, stressing each syllable. "It was just two chairs in front of a computer.... I had headphones on, and she would ask me what it said, and then I clicked pause, and then I'd read word for word what it said,... and I did it like—I think four days for an hour and a half." He eventually posted the transcript to WikiMarion alongside a videotaped version of the interview that he had edited and also burned to DVD.

At the end of the project, I asked Jason what he thought about having his work on WikiMarion. He replied:

> Everyone can see it—not just my classmates, not just school—everyone in the world can see.... They get to hear not only my perspective of [the lynching]. They get to hear my grandma's perspective of it and... my grandma being able to voice her opinions on the Internet to trillions, zillions of people. I think that thought she likes a lot.

I knew by this point that the interview with his grandmother had been a powerful experience, but I was surprised by this display of enthusiasm. Until the final days of the project, Jason had shown a relatively laid-back manner; certainly, he was not given to hyperbole. Yet he was clearly moved by the project and, as shown here, by the public nature of the work. He was pleased that the interview would be seen, as much on his grandmother's behalf as for himself. And while one might detect, in the phrase "zillions of people," adolescent visions of fame, this is balanced by an explicit statement of how the audience, too, would benefit. Many students simply stated that their work would provide people with information, but appropriately for an oral history, Jason specifies that the value is in presenting his grandmother's perspective.

Like Jason, the students adopted and endorsed, with near unanimity, the goal of doing work of public value. Of the nineteen participating students, fully eighteen of them mentioned that part of the project's value was that people would benefit from reading or using it. I do not claim that the students reached this interpretation independently. It is an implicit assumption of the CHP that students can do important public work, and my interviews were deliberately designed to probe whether students shared this goal and how they understood it. Still, the consistency of their responses and the sincerity and thoughtfulness of their analysis—all of which will become apparent in this chapter—suggest that this was a positive and powerful feature of the project.

Many students became convinced that their work was important. Speaking of their projects and the lynching, Tom and Emily used an identical phrase: "People need to know." Hannah said of the project, "It's information that needs to be out there for people to find.... It's important because it's there and people can access it now." The word "important" recurs throughout students' interviews and this chapter, as students used it to describe both their public projects and the knowledge they had gained. This was especially clear in the case of the student I call Zachary. At the beginning of the project, as we walked down the hallway before our introductory interview, Zachary announced, "There are people who don't want to hear the story, but it must be told."[3] I nodded and began to speak, but Zachary quickly cut me off. "Do you know who said those lines?... The character Frodo Baggins in a book by J. R. R. Tolkien, *The Lord of the Rings*." He explained that he had an interest in Christian literature and was quoting from one of his favorite books—and that he felt about the lynching as Frodo felt about the story of the ring. Zachary's project met with some obstacles, but this attitude persisted and deepened. Where he initially voiced a dramatic but unspecific commitment to showing the truth, in our final interview he said twice that his project "brought back into the light" certain groups that contributed to the lynching.

Other students developed a sense of obligation to their subjects or to the people who assisted their research. As we have seen with Jason and his grandmother, interviews seemed to promote this sort of connection. Biographies did as well. Emily became attached to her subject, Mary Ball, despite the fact that Ball was not an entirely sympathetic figure. Michael, who completed a project on lynching victim Thomas Shipp, told me, "We do this so his name and Smith's name will not just die… away because it's important for their names to live on and for this tragedy to never be forgotten." My research was initially motivated by the idea that "public value" might emerge as students' work products were consumed by an audience, and indeed, this is still the feature that distinguishes it most clearly from other forms of pedagogy. But as these statements suggest, value turns out to be a more complicated matter. The students became wrapped up in a complex web of importance, with feelings of obligation to their informants and research subjects and of a responsibility to tell important history, even though people might not always know that they need to hear it.

One way to characterize students' understanding of public value is in terms of their ability to articulate specific, realistic ways in which the public might benefit from their projects. Some noted only that people might "see" or "access" their work. Others had more clearly thought out the situations in which audience members might read their work and the ways in which they might learn from it. As a first example, consider Ben, who prepared a biographical page on Jake Campbell, the sheriff who ceded control of the county jail to the angry mob. I asked Ben, "What was good or bad about having your work end up on WikiMarion instead of just being handed in to the teacher for a grade?" He answered that when he turns work in to the teacher, "They're going to look over it and… it's going to sit there and collect dust and no one will ever be able to see it. But if I put it on the Internet, anyone in the world can see it… and my hard work gets shown off." This is in many ways an encouraging response, even as it is one that may echo language he had heard from me or Munn. Ben draws a sharp contrast between a typical assignment and this project, and he indicates that publicness makes the project more rewarding. However, in the quotation above, he speaks of this value in relationship to himself, without explanation of how others might benefit. A few minutes later, he restated the point with a greater emphasis on audience appreciation: "Not everyone is going to read my first semester [paper] and probably someone would like this [lynching project]." Even here, though, his explanation of how the public might benefit—what they might like—is limited in detail. Ben might have been capable of producing a more nuanced explanation if asked different questions, or he might have developed this ability with time, but he did not do so in the interview. Nick, who made a map of sites pertaining to the lynching, offered a similar response. Because his work is public, he said, "It shows… more than just my teacher that I put time and effort into this. You know, I went out of my way.… Honestly, I didn't think I'd ever see this [first-semester] paper again." At other points in the interview, Nick showed an inchoate sense that one can contribute to history.[4] Still, if we analyze statements in terms of the nuance in their explanation of public value, these quotations show certain limitations amid other, more promising signs.

Some students went further. Carmen, working with Hannah, created a wiki page about the lynching play *The Gospel According to James*. When I asked her, "What was good and bad about working on this project?" she responded, "What was good was that we could put something together to teach people that… don't know much about the lynching and interest them in the play." Jennifer responded similarly. Neither explanation is especially lengthy—these two were among the most soft-spoken interviewees—but in response to a very general question, both girls explicitly linked the value of their work to public learning. More than three-quarters of the students reached at least this level in explaining public value.

Many went still deeper. Three students believed not only that their work would inform the citizens of Marion but also that it might be built upon by future researchers. Caleb was one of several who uncovered important new resources, working on a lead that Munn and I put forward. As explained in Chapter 3, we had both heard that a retired administrator from Marion Community Schools, Carol Secttor, had once received a threatening letter from the Ku Klux Klan. As a young teacher in the 1970s, the story went, she tried to teach about the lynching and a few days later found a note in her mailbox—perhaps even a copy of the lynching photograph. After conferring with Munn, I suggested to students that someone might investigate, and Caleb jumped at the idea. The story was mostly true, he learned, except for its connection to the lynching. The letter had arrived after the teacher showed a video on the civil rights movement, and she had received a letter and Klan propaganda materials, but no photograph. Caleb scheduled an interview, and the administrator brought with her the materials, complete with the original envelope, offering to donate them. Caleb transcribed the interview, scanned the materials, uploaded some to a wiki page, and eventually deposited them at the public library's Indiana Room. He later told me that when reflecting on the project as a whole, he was most proud of the scanned documents—especially the ones with handwritten notes. The documents "could go to other projects," he explained, to "people who are just researching the Klan in the future," or possibly to "kids in the future who are doing local projects."

Caleb finished his project early and teamed with another student, Tom, to work on a front page for the wiki exhibit. They began to write an overview of the lynching with links to each piece of student work—each, that is, but Caleb's own, which was listed separately, as a "special project," because it was not directly related to the lynching. Having read a number of other student projects, the two acquired something of a bird's-eye view and a sense of the extent of what had been accomplished. Tom commented that the project was intended to help "the next generation to find out about" the lynching and remarked, "There's a lot more stuff that could be done. A lot more... and maybe over the years people will add more to it, which would be really cool." Tom, like Caleb, had a sense that the work was part of a larger effort, and he found the thought inspiring.

One project—Michael's biographical page on Thomas Shipp—explicitly built on research done by a previous student. Several years earlier, when Munn and a group of students had worked to restore the Weaver Cemetery south of town, each student had prepared a brief write-up about one person interred there. Shipp and Abram Smith, the two victims of the lynching, were among them. According to Munn, however, the physical restoration consumed the bulk of student time, and the Indiana Room director expressed disappointment with the Shipp and Smith projects, neither of which had been digitized. Munn occasionally allows students to extend or rework the projects of previous years, and this is what Michael did for Shipp. He expanded the project but also lamented the insufficiency of available sources, raising the possibility that in "future years my project will probably be redone maybe by somebody... [or] added on.... Maybe there's more information out there that I don't know about or... there's relatives out there that maybe somebody can get a hold of." Indeed, no breakthrough was made on the project that semester—important to keep in mind, in light of other striking successes—but Michael still displays something of a historian's sense of how knowledge is created over time.

For several students, the project's value lay in the fact that the lynching was local enough to allow for original work. This was apparent as Hannah compared her first- and second-semester projects. In December, she wrote about the Constitutional Convention, which she found "important because it's what our whole entire country stands on." She said of her wiki page, by contrast:

> The lynching project is valuable just because it's such a huge thing that happened in Marion, and very few people know more than the basics about it.... If I had to choose, I'd probably say the lynching one is more valuable just because information on [the] Articles of Confederation [and] Constitution are pretty easy for anyone to get hold of, whereas there's not a ton of information out there on the lynching.

For Hannah, a local project provides the opportunity to meet an unfulfilled need. For Julia, it allows for novel thinking: "So many people have written so many things about [the Louisiana Purchase, her first-semester topic]. All these theories have been proposed." But with the Marion lynching, "Not that many things have been proposed and you can just, kind of like, start new ideas." She developed some creative insights and tasted the excitement of original thought—an important and appealing feature of intellectual culture that is difficult to replicate when the curriculum hews to well-trodden historical ground.

For Hannah and Julia, the project's value owed to both localism and the opportunity to do work that might have interest outside the school. Julia added that the project might have broader import because of her unique relationship to the lynching: "I guess it's nice for some people to see a student, especially someone who grew up in Marion's perspective, which I think is pretty valuable." Her assessment was justified; James Madison, for one, had cited the reflections of an earlier generation of students in his book on the lynching. Subsequent events proved Julia right even more clearly. Four months later, as described in Chapter 3, a Northwestern professor expressed interest in the students' work and their perspectives on the event, and Julia was one of the students who met with him.

The students, then, saw a variety of forms of value in the project, including public learning, value to future researchers, and the ability to express a personal perspective. Partly on the strength of this motivation, many students reported working harder or more carefully than usual. I did not specifically ask about this issue, but they raised it time and again, especially when asked to compare their wiki projects with the papers they had written first semester. Weighing her first-semester paper on the Articles of Confederation against her second-semester project on Lawrence Beitler's lynching photograph, Alexis told me, "I feel like I did a much better job" on the latter. She said she did "thorough research" and "took more time to actually do this one and I just didn't throw it together in one night." Lynn explicitly linked her hard work to the responsibilities of publication: "I feel like it made me want to make it a little better and work a little harder on it for being on the wiki." Similarly, asked what advice he would give to new students embarking on this project, Eric admonished, "Don't dawdle. If it's being published, devote more time to it, proofread it.... Make sure that what you're saying makes sense, and it's just not your thoughts spewed onto a piece of paper." In all, more than half of the students said they worked harder or more carefully on this project or advised future students to do so because the work would be public.[5]

Two factors seem to be at play: Some student comments indicated that publicness made the work itself more valuable and more deserving of their effort. Others focused on the fact that when one's name is attached to public work, the quality of the work reflects on the author and could influence his or her reputation. The first of these can be seen, among other places, in a cluster of students who reported procrastinating less than usual on the project. Besides Alexis, who, as quoted above, "didn't just throw [her project] together in one night," two other students made similar comments. Michael told me,

> I'm just proud that I actually followed through and did all this the way that I did.... That's not usually me. That's not usually the kind of guy I am. Usually, I'm more of the procrastinator. I'll wait to the very last second to get it done, if I do get it done. And I actually started on this early,... came to the library often, and got as much information as I could.

According to Michael, the turning point came when he realized that he "could do something to provide a source for anybody." He mused, "Maybe a Shipp family member will come see this and appreciate what I did for him,... and that kind of gave me motivation to actually buckle down and do as much as I could." Similarly, Caleb told me that he often procrastinates but didn't on this project because "I felt like I'm actually learning something, and somebody else could use it in the future instead of just—you just do it and then it's gone." These students felt that the work was intrinsically interesting and important and merited their effort.

Along with these attractive features, however, publicness also presents certain risks. When I asked Ashley what was good and bad about having her work end up on WikiMarion, she said:

> Both good and bad I guess is that I know that other people are going to see it and that... it basically labels me because it's what I did.... So I guess maybe it made me

> work harder because of that, and [at] the same time it might have been a little bit of a stress. Like, "Oh no!" You want it to be good. You get perfectionistic when you know when your name is going to be on something.

Ashley demonstrates understanding that when work is to be public with her name attached, it will "label" her. Her sincere engagement with the project is clear throughout the interview, but she acknowledges that concern for her personal reputation also motivated her work. She adds the caveat that, from the student's perspective, this has the negative effect of adding stress.

Nearly half of the students expressed some trepidation about members of the audience finding mistakes in their work.[6] Among students, this was the most consistently mentioned downside of the project—the only one, in fact—though it was usually portrayed as a minor drawback that went hand in hand with other positive aspects. When I asked Samantha what was good and bad about having her work on WikiMarion, she replied, succinctly, "It's good because I want people to see the work and learn more. It's bad because I feel nervous if somebody is not going to like it." Alexis made an almost identical statement, also with the sense that public value and pressure are two sides of the same coin.

These comments took on their most negative cast with a student I call Eric. He, too, saw the positives in writing for a public audience, but he spoke more vividly about the "pressure" that wiki publication imposed. After exhorting future students to proofread their work carefully, he advised, "It's not just you that's going to see it. It's someone else, like a higher-up,... and you don't want to... jade your future because it's something that you didn't really care about." Eric appeared to be under more academic pressure than other students and also more sensitive to authority. In our introductory interview, I asked students to describe a typical weekend day in their lives. Whereas most mentioned hobbies or ways of relaxing, Eric told me about physics tutoring and homework. He repeatedly responded to my questions with "Yes, sir" and "No, sir," even when I asked him to call me by my first name. Eric was not complaining—simply commenting on the project as he experienced it. He seemed satisfied with the project in general, and this chapter includes a number of quotations that demonstrate his engagement. Still, to use familiar terms, his motivation seemed to be more extrinsic than intrinsic. Eric is certainly not the only high school student who feels a great deal of academic pressure. Four other students mentioned the impact their projects might have on college or similar applications, but all thought—sometimes after a moment's hesitation—that the public work would be a boon. Still, it is worth noting that students like Eric might experience it as another source of external pressure.

Within limits, this sort of pressure can be seen as a positive feature. When students learn in the process of creating public value, their work matters more, to them and others. My research suggests that this pushes them to work harder and more carefully, and with that comes a type of pressure that they are shielded from in more privately directed types of learning. There are situations in which private learning might be more appropriate, but I suspect that most teachers would welcome this sort of authentic, socially grounded motivation. In fact, teachers may themselves feel an added sense of motivation, a pride on students' behalf, and a need to hold students to high standards of work. Certainly this has been true for Munn.

Historical sophistication

Production-oriented forms of learning have often been faulted for lacking academic rigor. Diane Ravitch, for one, singles out the "hostility to subject matter" in Kilpatrick's (see Chapter 2) version of the project method (2000, p. 182), and similar criticisms have been made of *Foxfire*. In the project described here, while working to create valuable historical products, students engaged deeply with academic history. The evidence I will present indicates that students developed historical sophistication in a variety of forms, from knowledge, to research and writing skills, to their very conceptions of the nature of history. Not all students learned the same things, and what they did learn did not always align with state standards. But much of what they learned strikes me as important.

Most basically, the students developed knowledge of the subject matter at hand—the lynching and its context. I never specifically queried students about knowledge gains, but when I asked about the value of the project or about what they had learned, sixteen of the nineteen students included knowledge development in their answers. When I asked Eric, for example, what he was most proud of with regard to his wiki page, he cited "the knowledge I gained through this project." He went on to explain that at the beginning of the project, "I didn't know much, if anything, about lynching. So, looking back upon where I was then and where I am now, I felt as if I've gained a lot of knowledge about this event." This is not a statement made casually.

Eric compares his starting and end points, as if gauging the value added to his knowledge, and he judges the growth to be substantial. I did not, of course, measure this with actual pre- and post-tests. The sample size would have been small, and it would have been impossible to fairly measure student learning, given that they studied different topics. More substantively, the point of this research is to judge students by what they produced, not by what they could recall in a controlled environment. To a certain extent, the students' products demonstrate their knowledge development, showing what they understood well enough to use in research and writing. The students also showed their learning in presenting their work orally to the class, fielding questions, participating in discussions, and describing their projects in our final interviews.

Jason demonstrates, in several of these ways, the knowledge he developed in the course of preparing for and carrying out his interview with his grandmother. His learning is amply demonstrated in transcripts—both in the transcript of his interview with his grandmother and then in my closing interview with him. For example, when his grandmother struggled to remember the names of the lynching victims, Jason was able to supply them. In the course of researching the lynching, he developed other important knowledge that went beyond it. Looking back on the project in my final interview with him, Jason said, "I never knew that there were some African Americans that were fairly light-skinned and could pass as white back then because of their descent from slave owners and relationships with other female slaves." Moments later, he spontaneously mentioned having learned about the Underground Railroad in Marion—knowledge gained earlier in the year when Munn showed the class the documentary video made by a CHP student in 1998. Considering his overall learning, Jason said, "I never knew that I could edit a video like that.... I've never interviewed anyone like this, and I've never learned as much in two to three weeks as I did [then]." This was learning that exceeded expectations—mine and his.

The knowledge gained on this project was important to students because it impinged upon the communities that mattered to them. As Jason put it, when I asked what was valuable about the project, "It was something I *needed* to learn just because I'm African American myself. I need to know what happened to other African Americans in the history of Marion." It strikes me as rare and significant for a student to state with such conviction that he "needed to learn" academic subject matter. For Jason, the necessity of this learning stemmed both from the material's relationship to Marion and to African American history, but this chapter includes numerous examples of students from other backgrounds who felt the same way.

Lynn, too, found that local connections made the subject matter seem more important. She had written about the Boston Tea Party for her first-semester paper, and when I asked her the same question that I asked Jason—what was valuable about each project?—she compared them:

> The lynching project… was, I thought, more valuable because it's part of Marion's history, and… I've lived in Marion my whole life and I didn't know too much about it, and so now I do know more. And the Boston Tea Party I guess is pretty big history, too [*chuckles*], but I just don't really care for that as much, I guess.

Some students were more enthusiastic about their first-semester topics than Lynn was, but there was a general sense that the knowledge gained on their wiki projects was uniquely important and interesting.

Eighteen of the nineteen students used the word "interesting" or a close variant, and many used it repeatedly, describing Marion, their projects, or history in general.[7] When I asked Carmen for her feelings about history, she recalled our conversation at the project's outset: "At the beginning, when you were interviewing me, I said I didn't like history. But with doing this for research, I felt like I'm more interested in it now.… I think it's more important to learn about our country's history and just even here in Marion." Three students said the project was interesting because it was relevant; one said her particular topic related to her interests. But most commonly—just over half the time—their reasons were related to the topic being local. In comparing her first- and second-semester projects, Alexis said, "The Articles of Confederation, it was for everyone in America. [The lynching] just happened here in Marion. So I find it more intriguing." Tom, who lived near Lovers' Lane and researched it for the project, was interested by the proximity to his house, and he and two other students said the project "hit home" or was "close to home."

Only three students—Alex, Alexis, and Emily—failed explicitly to mention knowledge gains as a consequence of their second-semester projects. In each case, the students' projects demonstrate ample knowledge development—indeed, these are among the deepest, most information-rich projects of the group—but the students themselves tended to talk about their learning in more complex ways. For example, Alex, Bill Munn's son, cited knowledge when speaking of his first-semester project. He stated that this paper, on the XYZ Affair, "was valuable to me in the sense that I learned a lot more about the early United States international affairs than I would have known otherwise." But he spoke of his project on the memorialization of lynching in terms that were far more sophisticated and personally meaningful. From the beginning of the project, Alex showed a streak of intellectual activism, like his father, and a concern about racial divisions and inequality. Earlier in the year, he had written several letters to the editor of the *Chronicle-Tribune* about school-related issues. He enjoyed history but at the same time looked more toward a career in science and technology, and when the project began, he professed to have only a limited knowledge of the lynching and his father's work. With several other students, he saw *The Gospel According to James* and became upset by the absence of a lynching memorial in Marion. He was convinced that a memorial would be beneficial and undertook a project that would determine why none existed. This optimism was short lived, however. With his father's guidance—but not, so far as I could tell, his pressure, which would likely have provoked Alex's resistance—he delved into the history of reconciliation efforts in Marion and dived into databases such as LexisNexis and Google Books to learn from other communities dealing with similar atrocities, from Duluth, Minnesota, to Rosewood, Florida. By the third week of the project, he approached me after class saying, "I've had a change of heart on this issue. This sounds cynical, but I think we can't correct what [the lynching] has done. This lynching happened, and it has divided Marion."[8]

Alex vacillated for a time, torn between what he characterized as cynicism and his activist inclination that something might be done. His resolve was also bolstered by successes in other areas of the project, such as his acquisition of a collection of documents from the 2003 reconciliation events. Eventually he settled on the following argument, as phrased in his paper: "For true progress in our local racial dialogue, the memorial of the lynching must reflect an understanding of this generation's responsibility to account for their forefather's crime. Without such, it serves to do little." In our final interview, Alex commented on the value of this process, saying that it "was really beneficial to me because it stopped the swinging back and forth of pessimism to optimism." The project offered an extended opportunity to work out ideas he felt to be deeply important, eventually bringing them to some measure of resolution. The work built on his existing commitments and inclinations, but it also facilitated a substantial maturation in his view of the world—a tempering of initial optimism and a more subtle and realistic view of what historical study can achieve.

Exactly what students learned varied among projects. Just as their research led them to different subject matter, it also called upon different research skills. Those who spent time in the archives learned in a manner different from those who conducted interviews or spent more time with secondary sources.

One of the more archive-intensive projects was completed by Ashley, the devout Christian who told me she had been called to be a missionary. Ashley researched the role of the church in the lynching and in later reconciliation efforts. On the evening of May 12, she visited the Marion Public Library, frustrated by her lack of sources. She talked first to Betty Reynolds, the library staff member who had assembled the binders of lynching articles, and when I first checked in, she was leafing through them. She had previously read relevant sections from Cynthia Carr's *Our Town* (2006), and I pointed out where Carr had quoted from the articles she was reading, mentioning at the same time that Ashley might choose different quotations to support her own argument. She replied, "I'm actually excited to write this now."

Ashley's final interview confirmed her excitement. Looking back on the project, she reflected, "To really have such firsthand articles... is different and it's fun.... Instead of just being given the facts... you are piecing the true facts and figuring out how that fits. They're all just little pieces of the puzzle and then you have to fit them together yourself." Her comment highlights the active, critical thought that the project required. I count this as a strength, but this alone could be replicated in a classroom by giving students a collection of documents to analyze. Ashley goes further, noting that the wiki page "gave me a chance to do my own research in a way that I never really got a chance to do before in a project. To find my own thing, discover things on my own." Her pride was not solely in piecing things together, but also in a larger ownership of the project. The project was very deeply her own, as she reckoned with the church's culpability in the racial and cultural climate of the 1920s. She also describes this as a new experience, despite the fact that she had spent the year in a history class that emphasized writing, critical thinking, and documentary analysis. This project added something important that had not been covered in the rest of the curriculum.

Ashley was not alone in this experience. Lynn, Ben, and David all worked extensively with original documents, and all expressed similar understandings. David told me it was "unique to draw your own conclusion of what you thought happened that night and the surrounding events.... If you watched a video about it, you just get what they told you about it. By doing your own research, you are able to see and come to your own conclusions and thoughts." Ben, too, said of this type of research, "It's not... clear, you have to make inferences for yourself and you... gather information." Like Ashley, both David and Ben emphasize the active thought required by the project and the way it engendered in them a heightened sense of intellectual independence.

Students drew a variety of lessons from this experience, often about the need for evidence to support their arguments and about how to navigate the archive and make sense of its contents. In the course of creating a map of places important to the lynching, Nick developed a firm commitment to supporting his locations with evidence drawn from city directories, census records, and newspaper articles. He told me with a hint of exasperation that Mr. Munn continually suggested, offhand, new locations that he might include on his map. Nick said, "I'm like, 'Well I have to have exact information on it. You know, like, a source or a cite.'" A student might approach citations as a requirement imposed by a teacher, but Nick internalized an ethic of evidence. He presented himself as standing up to the teacher, insisting on documentation. Nick's project was far from perfect. For one, it seemed to me that he sometimes trusted the wrong sources. When attempting to identify the home address of Mary Ball, he used an address from a 1929 City Directory despite the fact that 1930 newspaper coverage listed the family at a new address—and even though they were listed at the same new address in the 1931 directory. (The year 1930 was missing from the collection.) I pointed this out several times, and he eventually changed the address, but more on the force of my authority than his own judgment. In the closing days of the year, Nick was repeatedly absent, and his finished product did not fulfill all of my expectations, but the project was a highly positive experience, and Nick developed both a basic understanding of evidence and a personal commitment to corroboration.

David showed at least as much commitment to his evidence and spoke about it in greater depth. An aspiring attorney, David researched the lynching's legal aftermath, and the process proved interesting but also disheartening in several ways. Four alleged members of the mob were tried and acquitted, and at some point in the ensuing decades the transcripts had disappeared. The library did have a set of depositions from a justice of the peace inquest (also known as the Court of Inquiry), and David was able to work with these, but as he read through transcript after transcript, he found in each the same evasions. One by one, witnesses claimed not to have recognized any mob members. David hoped to find someone who broke ranks but never did, an experience he described as "grim." Having made no headway in identifying the perpetrators, he set out to demonstrate a concerted cover-up and collective responsibility. David wrote:

> Roy Collins, the assistant chief of police, was the first in a long line of witnesses. He was questioned many times for any information that could lead to establishing the identities of the mob leaders.

Q: Were the lights sufficiently strong there for you to have distinguished and recognized the features of any one?
A: I don't believe they were, if they were I didn't see them; I am telling you the fact, I couldn't tell you a soul that was there.[9]

He cited three of the thirty depositions, showing something of the consistency of the evasions.

David had transferred to Marion at the beginning of the year, and teachers at his previous school had not required the use of citations. The requirement sometimes frustrated him; when we discussed his first-semester paper, he said the most difficult thing was learning to use Turabian citation form. But regarding his wiki project, he explained clearly the need for citing the various depositions. "If I didn't have them in here, there'd be no evidence to back up anything I was saying, really. I could have just made up Roy Collins.... It just shows that there's evidence with what I've said. There's basis for what I'm saying. It's not just out of the blue."

David had a purpose in writing and chose evidence to support his argument. Historian James Madison (2001) had analyzed the depositions in *A Lynching in the Heartland*, citing testimony from Sheriff Campbell, but David had quoted from different witnesses. He explained the choice: "Jake Campbell is not as important for what I was trying to do.... I was trying to prove that the community was involved in it." Note that he had a clear sense of his own purpose, was comfortable differentiating his analysis from that of the leading expert on the event, and appreciated that different arguments call for different evidence. David cited Madison's analysis on points on which they agreed, explaining, "If I draw from more than one source, it would feel like a more complete picture because more than one [person] could come to that conclusion." It is unclear to what extent these understandings developed during the project or predated them, but as quoted above, he did appreciate that the project provided a "unique" opportunity to "draw your own conclusion."

Emily, like David, talked about evaluating the reliability of sources. Her project focused on Mary Ball, who leveled the rape accusation that precipitated the lynching. Emily's research process started slowly, as she turned up a few documents and census records but little new information. Mary Ball had disappeared from Marion in the years after the lynching, and her later life was long a mystery. In the final weeks of the semester, however, Emily's research came together. She contacted James Madison, who introduced her to a woman who had known Ball in California in the 1970s and 1980s. Ball had married a man with grown children, and this woman, Madeline Patterson, was married to Ball's stepson. The rest of Ball's family had denied interview requests, but Patterson had since divorced the stepson and was willing to talk. She had previously talked with both Madison and Cynthia Carr, but Emily hoped she could provide information not yet in the public record.

Emily emailed Madeline Patterson a few short questions, and the responses began to roll in—six lengthy messages over several days, plus some shorter correspondence. She seemed to bear no animus toward Mary Ball, and the emails contained useful information about Ball's career, family life, and personality. At the same time, her tone was breathless, and one of the details she insisted on most strongly was the most far fetched—that she had felt some sort of paranormal presence the night of Mary's death. Emily read them with her mother, who found them credible at times but "didn't know whether to believe some of the stuff," in part because of Patterson's advancing age. In class a few days later, Munn, Emily, and I had a similar conversation about what information could be trusted. Ultimately, she omitted some of Patterson's stories but judged her account mostly believable, partly because she compared the information with Carr's version of events and verified that "stuff matched up." As best I understand, Emily found it reassuring that Patterson had told the same story years earlier—presumably important because she was younger and closer in time to the events—and that her story was also corroborated by some of Carr's other sources. The situation is complicated, but Munn and James Madison both approved of Emily's judgment.

This is an important lesson in historical practice, and Emily seemed to grasp the basic principle and to have learned it while doing real historical activity in a knotty, ill-structured case with real import. To this point, I have described experiences in which, in the course of their research, Nick, David, and Emily needed to evaluate sources and corroborate among them. The experience was fairly common among students whose projects involved work with documentary evidence—which is not to say that all did it as successfully.[10] As an example of less critical reading, in Chapter 5 I discuss Michael's reliance on James Cameron's (1982/1994) account as a historical source, with which some members of the public appropriately took issue. I was encouraged by Michael's sense of contribution to the Shipp family and am hopeful that with further value-creating work and adult guidance, his skill would improve. Still, it is important to keep in mind that there are limits to student historiography.

Julia, although she approached knowledge in a more critical way, did not always deploy it successfully in her written work. Her research dealt with lynching as a national phenomenon, situating the Marion event within larger patterns of racial violence. The librarians and I directed her to a number of secondary works on file in the Indiana Room, but she latched onto a book from Munn's personal collection, Orlando Patterson's *Rituals of Blood: Consequences of Slavery in Two American Centuries* (1998). In the sections that interested her most, Patterson interpreted lynching first in light of the history and sociology of human sacrifice and then in the context of the culture of the American South after the Civil War. I was present one evening in the Indiana Room as Julia conducted the research. She sat with several other students, and I sat across the room, monitoring the scene but giving the students room to work. Julia read through the brief accounts of lynchings that ran in Marion's newspapers in the 1920s, noticing patterns and intersections with Patterson's analysis and coming to me excited with each new discovery. She was struck by Patterson's observation that in cases of ritual violence and sacrifice, the taking of life is often followed by silence—just as it was in Marion, when James Cameron was spared. She took these as explanations for certain features of the Marion lynching, arguing that it was influenced both by newspaper articles in the years before 1930 and the "deeply ingrained human sacrificial human nature."

For me, this was one of the most invigorating moments of the project. As I have mentioned, Julia would later remark on the excitement of being able to "start new ideas," capturing a sense of novelty that is rarely present in a traditional high school paper. But the promise was not always realized in Julia's written product. In her write-up, she outlined this basic observation but cited only one article from the binders she had examined that evening. The article was taken from an Evansville newspaper, in southern Indiana, and Julia said merely that the headline was "blatantly racist." This was true enough, but it did not directly support her point, and it did not do justice to the more creative insights she initially expressed. She also struggled, understandably, to write about Orlando Patterson's (1998) complex ideas. One of the more sociologically astute students in the class, Julia comprehended them in at least a basic way and found them exciting. She struggled to articulate them, however, especially with enough clarity for a public audience. This sort of paper, more conceptually demanding and with a complicated argument, would have benefited from another round of feedback and additional time to revise.

It was evident, as students talked about their projects, that they were tailoring their writing for public audiences. Reflecting on his first-semester paper in our interview, Tom recalled, "I was writing with one specific person in mind... Mr. Munn." But thinking of the second-semester wiki project, he observed that there is a "different way you work on things when it's meant not just for your teacher to look at, but for the public." He said he had attempted to write the lynching project "in a way that everybody will be able to identify with," whereas on his first paper for Munn, he wrote at a "higher level... of education," using "much more flowery language." Writing for the wiki, then, he had modulated the register of his writing to meet the perceived needs of the audience.

Ashley was more concerned with the amount of background knowledge she could assume from her readers. Like Tom, she began by noting that her first-semester paper "was more of a paper written to Mr. Munn." By contrast, she continued:

> The WikiMarion page,... that was more for people who really don't know what's going on [with the lynching].... It's written to your community to learn more about it. So, it's written more in a broader scope, so that if they stumbled across that page they could understand the lynching, they could understand Marion's history a little better.

Ashley not only showed an awareness of her audience but also said her work was intended to help its members learn. She had clearly given some thought to her readers and imagined a plausible scenario in which someone could encounter her page. Realizing that such a person might know nothing about the event, she provided necessary contextual information.

David agreed on all counts. Like Tom, he was aware that on the web, he had no captive audience: "Because this is going on WikiMarion, you have to obviously make it a little bit more interesting so that people will want to read it." Like Ashley, he noted that his WikiMarion project had "a lot more context to it" than did his first-semester paper on the Treaty of Ghent. "If you don't have a general understanding of the Treaty of Ghent or the War of 1812," he said, "you're not really going to be able to understand what's going on in this paper." With his lynching project, on the other hand, "You could not even really know about the fact that the Marion lynching even happened" and still follow the argument.

The project introduced students to new ways of interacting with history—conducting original research for the purpose of creating public products of some consequence. Several were struck by how little they understood, in spite of their research. As Michael commented:

> When I think of the past, it kind of bothers me because that's something that I could never experience.... Because there's only so much we can know without actually being in there and experiencing it.... And that's kind of frustrating in a way I guess. You could never have the complete truth.

Michael may not have developed this insight on his own; I suspect he was repeating an idea he had heard elsewhere. But he spoke of frustration, and not merely in some abstract sense. As the context of the interview makes clear, he connected it to his difficulty in finding sources on Thomas Shipp—and locating original documents beyond birth and death records was a legitimate struggle. It was surprising that he said this, given the certainty with which his project restated Cameron's story and also because Michael had, to that point, been relatively matter-of-fact. As a teacher, I hoped this statement represented an inchoate historical understanding that could be brought out in subsequent work.

Where Michael was struck by the incompleteness of his sources, Ashley ruminated on the increasing depth of her knowledge: "History is not super easy. It's not just laid out and we don't know all the facts, and so to hear all the different opinions and get the resources.... It's a lot more complicated. The more you know, the more you realize that." For Tom, increasing knowledge of history made his understanding more vivid: "The more you into look at it, the more real it becomes.... It was not just people sitting on their butts in log houses." When I asked Ashley for a word to describe history, she sighed and said, "confusing," remarking on the "diversity" of history before settling on the word "complexity."

Hannah, whose project experience I relate in the next and final section of the chapter, developed a strong appreciation of this complexity and saw in it the potential for increased tolerance. "Maybe to people that have always been taught... one way—like they've grown up thinking, 'It's all this person's fault'... it explains that maybe things are not as definite as they always thought they were. So I'd say that can be helpful." Hannah's perspective might have been attributable, in part, to her attendance at *The Gospel According to James*, which conveyed ambiguity and gestured, albeit implicitly, toward the themes she addressed. Michael and Ashley, quoted above making similar statements, did not see the play. Many students came to see history not as an inert body of facts but as functioning in their world and especially as a tool for racial reconciliation.

Several voiced what appears to be a paraphrase of Santayana's axiom, "Those who cannot remember the past are condemned to repeat it." Ashley said the project could help the community "simply to understand the history better so that we can have a better future." She continued, "If you don't look at the past, you are going to make the same mistakes. It's good to see what really happened and not trying to hide anything, but be honest about what's going on and what we need to do to improve things." Similarly, Julia said that working on the project "makes you more sensitive to racial issues and makes you really not want to repeat the past and, just, change things." In our opening interview, Eric took a more pessimistic position, alluding to the same axiom but stipulating, "From the mistakes that I've seen made in the world, we haven't necessarily learned from our mistakes."

When I asked Nick to describe history, he compared history class with math class. "In history, you can go out and... find the answer as opposed to math we have to go and do the answer" or "figure out the answer." He attempted several times to state this in different ways, seeming to sense a distinction that lay beyond his immediate grasp. He never articulated it with complete clarity, but the distinction seemed to rest on a sense of history as open-ended rather than predetermined. Nick finally described the field as one where "you go out and you make the answer," saying, as an illustration:

> If you were to go out and just, you know, like, "I'm going to build a memorial to some so-and-so." Okay, I mean, that's part of history. You just made a memorial to someone or something that is in history, but you're part of it... just making a memorial. Part of today.

In these quotations, one can see Nick working out an understanding of history as a field that people participate in creating—not only by constructing personal understandings but also by contributing to public historical memory.

Alex, too, saw history as a participatory matter and presented his work as a sort of intellectual activism: "What I really hoped to do is to define the necessity of accountability and how the reconciliation is a springboard to this." As he thought the issue over, he repeated three times that his goal was to "define the issue" in terms of collective accountability. Paradoxically, he also noted that he did not see much of an audience for his paper, saying, "I don't know that I envision many people reading it.... I don't feel like the people of Marion are particularly proactive about even education," or, he implied, social change. Alex's comments were unusually sophisticated, but they demonstrated a sort of reasoning that might be achieved by a good student with sustained public engagement and reflection.

Personal development

To this point, I have focused on the ways in which the students who participated in this project advanced in their historical knowledge and practice and in their conceptions of the nature of the discipline. It should be clear that the project also engaged students like Alex at a more personal level. Many students found this work interesting and valuable in part because it addressed the history of the place where they lived, and this personal connection can be seen as more than a mere motivational bonus. Gottlieb and Wineburg have proposed that historical learning be conceived of as developing along and between two axes: first, increasing disciplinary sophistication, which is the more commonly recognized of the two, and second, negotiation of a learner's personal and communal commitments, with the goals of providing "engagement with a history that matters" and "produc[ing] a citizenry that is neither hopelessly gullible nor irredeemably cynical" (2012, p. 116). Endorsing those goals, I add that one way of coming to appreciate why history matters is by contributing to the history of communities of which one is a member. In this section, I discuss the sorts of personal and often communal learning that were on display in the students' lynching research and that sometimes brought personal commitments into contact with critical history. Judging by the evidence gathered in interviews and the work itself, the project did engage students at a personal level, calling on them to work in ways that engaged and impinged on their commitments and relationships—particularly in terms of race, religion, family, and the broader Marion community.

One indication that the project engaged students in personal ways was the regularity with which they mentioned talking about it with members of their families. Just over two-thirds of the students told me that they showed their work to family members or discussed the lynching with them in the context of their class projects.[11] In some cases, the interactions between students and parents seemed fairly typical of a school project—the parent looked at the student's work and praised it. But in other cases, the project led to more meaningful conversations. Ashley learned, midway through her project on the 2003 reconciliation events, that her mother had taken part in them, praying for their pastor who was also involved. Another student talked with her mother and grandfather, the latter of whom had owned a copy of the photograph. Although I was unable to learn anything more about this conversation, because of the sensitivity of the issue and the student's general reticence, the confluence of the topic, the familial relationship, and the student's academic research points to an encounter of weight and significance.

In some cases, family members provided a test bed in which students gauged public knowledge of the lynching. Said Samantha, "When I talked to my mom about it ... she didn't really know much.... And then I told her the story. And, I mean, she has lived here almost her whole life." Samantha's comment suggests a hint of surprise that her mother would not know more about such an important event. For other students—Hannah, Jennifer, Julia—relatives served as editors or members of a first audience. Julia showed a draft of her paper to her college-age sisters, who "tore it apart" but also were "surprised" and impressed by the ideas. "They don't think their little sister is intellectual, I guess," she said with satisfaction. Carmen showed her project on *The Gospel According to James* to her younger brother. She told me, "He learned a little bit from it, too, because he didn't know much about [the lynching] either. He is younger than I am, and he is, like, 'Oh, I didn't know this happened.' And... he was like, 'I kind of want to go see the play.'" For Samantha and Carmen, family members provided confirmation that their projects were of wider interest, in that their relatives knew little but were interested to learn more.

Familial interactions can also present an opportunity for students to consider how school subject matter relates to their own place in society. Jason, after working for most of the project with his grandmother alone, eventually shared it with his parents as well. "They were proud of me that I put my mind into something like this," he reported. "For them as... African American parents, it makes them feel good that their son, who they haven't really explained much to about this, took responsibility for something like this." Parental pride is welcome, even heart warming, but taken by itself would do little to distinguish this project from others. What is more important is the way Jason links their pride, in light of the incident being studied, to African American community membership and identity. We have already seen Jason's enthusiasm for reaching a generalized audience of "zillions of people," but these last comments indicate that he also saw himself as performing a service that befitted and fulfilled his role in the family and in relation to his African American identity.

This project engaged student identities of several types, including, as we will see, race, religion, and region. Julia's project called on a different sort of racial identity—her position as a person of mixed race—and touched upon issues of gender as well. With two weeks left in the project, we sat and discussed a draft of her work. She had recently read Orlando Patterson (1998), as described above, and was struck by Patterson's comments on the history of race and sexuality in the American South. As we discussed this on an intellectual level, she interrupted to offer a personal anecdote about a trip to a nearby town notorious as a hotbed of racism: "I've even been to Elwood with my parents before and they can just tell that my parents were interracial and they were just glaring.... And they were just disgusted by the fact that she's Chinese, he's white." She went on to discuss attitudes toward interracial dating among her friends and their parents, some of whom were supportive, while others disapproved. In our final interview, I asked whether she had thought any more about the issue, and she replied, "I started paying more attention to interracial relations like between friends or like boyfriend–girlfriend, and I realized that we've come a long way.... A lot of people are interracially friends or boyfriend and girlfriend." Julia's reflections contained no outright epiphanies, and the idea that "we've come a long way," while true, sometimes underplays the ongoing legacies of older divisions and injustices. But importantly—and positively, from my perspective—the research impinged on her life outside of school, inviting her to look at present-day social practices in historical context.

Some of the students' deepest reflections came when they considered the relationship between Christianity and the lynching, often in the context of their own faith. Especially clear in this regard were comments made by Hannah, the daughter of a Wesleyan pastor. Hannah was affected profoundly as she realized that the lynching story involved a church near her home:

> When I found out that the people met at a church to organize it, that *really*, really bothered me.... Alan Beck, the guy [Carmen] interviewed, he was showing us a picture of the box company [where some mob members worked] and the church that they met at. And I realized that the church was right next to my house.... Two streets over is this church and I've seen it before and I've seen the box company. And just the idea that a church that's supposed to be the place where Christians and loving people meet and then that's where they organized such an awful, disgusting—

She paused briefly and then attempted to complete the thought, but she could not, seeming to have reached a momentary limit of comprehension. Hannah had been taught that the Wesleyan Church was formed by abolitionists who split from the Methodist Church over slavery, and she mused, "You would think that Marion, which is so heavily Wesleyan everywhere, you would think that churches would be more against something like that." There is some truth to the historical point about the evangelical denomination's anti-slavery roots, but if this is the primary thrust of the church's teaching about its historical relationship to race, it is a highly selective history. Brought face-to-face with the other side of the story, Hannah came to a more complex view:

> Obviously there are churches out there that aren't just godly, loving, love everyone places.... You can't always look at something and know definitely, like, "Oh these people are going to be good" or, "Oh these people are going to be bad."... You can't just assume because they're a church that they are going to be against something like this because obviously they weren't all.

This assessment is balanced and sober. The project exposed Hannah to a more critical perspective on race and Christianity that gave her great pause and left her with a more nuanced understanding of her religious tradition.

Even as the project provoked much surprise and reflection on religious matters, students in their written work often pulled back from the brink, interpreting events in ways that reflected their preexisting commitments and showed less critical consideration than might have been warranted. Reading Ashley's project on the church and the lynching, one historian thought her too generous toward her own religious tradition. The situation is complicated, and I will address it in the following chapter, but ultimately it shows both learning, the limits of high school students' historiography, and the larger tension, not limited to the young, between commitment and critical thought.

The personal connections made by students were not always so lofty and sometimes simply involved comparisons between their own lives and lives led in 1930 Marion. Asked to describe history, Emily said, "I like history a lot more now than I did, just because of this project." She went on to explain, "I never used to like history that much. I mean, I'm not good with dates and everything.... It's just interesting, everything that I found out, it's kind of like... a reality show [*chuckles*]... [and] that's what I watch on TV." Emily's project was long on this sort of intrigue. Her subject, Mary Ball, was at the center of the murder and rape allegations that precipitated the lynching, and rumors circulated about Mary and her possible romantic involvement with several of the men involved in the events. Ultimately, Emily's research brought her into direct contact with an acquaintance of Mary Ball's. She emerged from this experience with a strong sense that history involved real people and relationships and was relevant to her own interests and tastes.

Similarly, Jason learned from his grandmother that some people mistook the lynch mob for a high school sports rally. An athlete himself, Jason remarked, "I never knew that back then they had little rallies and stuff like that. I didn't know people back then were as social as we are now.... I just thought they had more discipline." It may come as a surprise that a student could hear this story and focus on such a seemingly trivial detail, but as I have shown, Jason did not sidestep weightier issues. The point is that even when reckoning with a deep and troubling topic such as racial violence, the students also interpreted history in light of more commonplace aspects of their identities, and that these mundane details can also make historical figures seem more recognizably human. Much as with Emily, this helped Jason see the citizens of 1930 Marion not as sepia-toned paragons of "discipline" but as people with lives in some ways similar to his own.

Occasional digressions notwithstanding, the students' focus remained largely on the lynching and surrounding events, usually with an appropriately somber tone. As I have mentioned, David spoke of having a "grim feeling" as he read trial depositions. Emily remarked on how "sad" and "upsetting" the material was and also described a critical moment in her own project, when she exchanged emails with Mary Ball's California stepdaughter:

> It was just a lot to take in, everything that she sent me... because she was saying how [Mary Ball] acted... around people. Her and her husband slept in different rooms. They never bore children.... [It] was hard to take in all of it at once. And then, also reading Carr's book at the same time.

This sort of emotional saturation cropped up several times in interviews. Jennifer was "overwhelmed" by sadness when watching *The Gospel According to James*. Alex said it was "overwhelming," in a more positive sense, when an organizer of the 2003 reconciliation presented him with an overflowing binder of his personal documents. Jason said that researching the lynching was "like reliving it in my mind."

Surprisingly, and sometimes confoundingly, the project also evoked certain positive feelings—of interest, importance, and pride in place and progress made. Especially at the beginning of the project, some of the students made comments to indicate that they had little attachment to the city and felt only a weak sense of place, but during our final interviews, nearly half of the students specifically mentioned that Marion was more interesting and important than they had realized.[12] Carmen told me, "There's so many things that can still be discovered from here. Even if it's like a small town [and] nobody wants to be here. There's a lot of interesting and important things that happened here." Jason said that Marion "has somewhat more of an importance to me because I know what went on in the past." When I interviewed Eric at the beginning of the project, I asked him to describe the town. "Isolated," he replied. At the project's conclusion I asked this question again. "Boring," he began, almost reflexively, but he quickly thought better: "I guess not that boring now that I know more about the lynching. I guess it's kind of exciting to say, 'Oh, Marion was kind of a big place for history, for black history, because of this happening.'" It is interesting that Eric, an African American student, would consider this to be "black history"—surely it is at least as much a matter of white history. But students of all racial and ethnic backgrounds found the event powerful.

The students differed in how they thought about the event in relation to modern Marion. Eric, who also described history as "slightly interesting, sad, enraging, enlightening," said of the lynching, "I'm kind of angry at Marion for letting this happen." He absolved the town's modern-day residents, but only conditionally: "I guess the past is the past.... Just so long as it doesn't happen again, then I guess they can be forgiven for something that none of these... people of today did." Eric's grudging forgiveness indicates a reluctance to put history behind him, but others drew a much sharper line between past and present. Caleb told me that after the project, he had "more respect" for Marion "because of what it's been... and how it's come along." Michael told me, "I would say we've come a long way, but Marion was definitely a *very* bad place."

Roughly a third of the students voiced some variant of this idea, and it was difficult for me to decide what to make of it.[13] For one thing, I had much the same thought as Hannah, who said, "For the most part, how things were done and how people acted and thought then... is very different than how people are in [the] Marion that I live in now." The school seemed relatively harmonious, and the city and county have a long and admirable tradition of African American civic leadership. For another thing, appreciating differentness can also represent a kind of sophistication. After seeing Klan propaganda from the 1970s, Caleb was surprised that this kind of racism had persisted so long and said, "Marion was more interesting than I kind of thought it was. It had... a different history. I figured it's just always been the same." Rather than seeing the town as eternal and unchanging, Caleb noted the difference between past and present in a way that indicated an emerging historical understanding. Still, I had hoped—perhaps underestimating the incomprehensible otherness of a lynch mob or the power of a redemption narrative—that students would be quicker to recognize the many cultural and economic inequities that remained and to see them in continuity with the past.

Some of the students' positive sentiments may reflect a spill-over effect from the rest of the CHP, which operates on the tacit assumption that local history instills pride and a sense of place. One of the strongest examples of this came from Ashley, and it came as she talked not about the lynching project but about the presentations in which other class members (non-participants in the research) told stories of Marion High School alumni and local veterans. Ashley said, "There's so much more... history to people that you don't really think about before." She cited one interview that a classmate had conducted with one of their teachers and another with the father of a close friend. The latter interview gave Ashley the sense that she was encountering someone on a deeper level than she ever had before. "It's strange how you can know someone," she ruminated. "I know him really well. Since I was like in third grade. But to hear all that he's done, like in the Vietnam War... and being in Germany when the wall came down.... It's like [*whispering*] Wow!"

These interviews impressed upon Ashley a sense of pride in her community. "It's amazing to see.... Small little Marion, it seems so tiny and insignificant when you think about the whole country. But to hear these different stories, of locating enemy planes and saving American lives, They did... big things." Ashley said, "Before this project, honestly I never really felt about Marion as a community.... I just thought more in a worldly bigger picture." Her project on the reconciliation events gave her a sense of "pride" and made her see that Marion "isn't just a name that goes on my address." Instead, "It's an actual town and actually has history." It was as if she had moved to a new place—more exciting, less innocent, still worthy of respect—and it seemed unlikely that this change would be reversed.

Value and point of view

Among many signs of educational success, one feature of the students' interview answers gave cause for concern, pointing to a limitation of the project and an underlying tension regarding value, argument, and point of view. I have discussed at some length the ways in which this project gave students occasion to learn about issues of personal importance and, at times, to refine their own positions on those issues. I was surprised, then, to find that at least a few students did not believe the project called on them to make arguments, especially when compared with traditional history papers. Tom said, of his own wiki page, "[It's] less that you're writing a paper where you're trying to get a point across." For him and others, the issue was largely about eradicating "bias." While peer editing with David, he explained, the two spent time "making sure that everything's as unbiased as possible so we can get the most to the people without it being... contaminated, in a sense, by our own views." Note, in particular, the way he interpreted public edification—getting "the most to the people"—as being in conflict with expressing personal opinion, and that this seemed to inform his sense that the work did not require developing a "point." In credit to Tom, it is true that one purpose of these projects was to inform. Likewise, there is virtue in being faithful to evidence, aware of one's own biases, and open to alternative explanations. But my argument rests on the premise that personal views should hardly be thought of as *contaminating* one's work and are, in fact, integral to understanding and writing about history.

Tom began the project with many of these concerns already in mind, drawing sharp boundaries between fact, argument, and storytelling as early as our first interview. Upon reading James Madison's introduction to *A Lynching in the Heartland*, Tom was annoyed by the historian's opening statement, which reads: "This is a book about race. It masquerades as a book about a lynching" (2001, p. 1). It was not that he objected to Madison's point. On other occasions, he had no trouble acknowledging that the lynching was motivated by racial hostility. But he was only interested in learning the facts of the case, unadulterated by larger arguments or agendas. A few days after that first interview, upon seeing *The Gospel According to James*, Tom was impressed but also troubled by the comingling of fact and "storytelling." We discussed the matter at some length, and he conceded that argument and storytelling have their place, but he preferred that they be kept separate, and his sympathies consistently lay on the side of concrete fact. As best I can determine, the project was not the source of Tom's beliefs about fact, argument, and narrative, but it also did little to dispel or clarify them with regard to the study of history. It may, in fact, have reinforced them, in that it allowed Tom to make sense of the new experience in light of those preexisting conceptions.

There was variation among student interpretations of the relationship between fact and value, and, indeed, even within Tom and David's peer-editing pair. Whereas Tom preferred to keep personal positions out of the equation, David took a different view. He advised students beginning a similar project, "Don't approach it unemotionally, like you would a normal history paper, like I did with the Treaty of Ghent paper." He viewed his wiki writing as a matter of balancing competing concerns: "It's a very tragic event... and you have to handle something like that carefully. You don't want to go in there being entirely apathetic to it, unemotional, and sound indifferent to the whole incident. You want to have some emotion in it but you also don't want to go too far." David's inclination to seek a balance among conflicting concerns struck me as one of the most thoughtful and mature of the student reflections.

Other students, though, shared Tom's concern with eliminating point of view. Ashley described her project as "more about helping people understand the topic, not really understanding a point I'm trying to prove." Zachary, despite invoking Tolkien in defense of his moral commitments, said that in his paper he tried to "leave out anything that would bring out my opinions." Julia counseled future students, "Don't let your own morals get into play when you're writing a paper." To illustrate, she alluded to James Cameron's (1982/1994) insistence that a voice from heaven had quelled the mob and saved his life. "I'm religious but I didn't accept James Cameron's claim as being the truth," she said. In this particular case, Julia's judgment was entirely appropriate, and there was something admirable in her and her classmates' commitment to fair-minded inquiry. But her project was also fraught with moral implications. This was the young woman who reflected on interracial relationships and her own mixed-race family and who saw her perspective, having grown up in the lynching town, as a source of her project's value. At the very least, this seems to call for a more nuanced understanding of "morals" than her blanket dismissal implies.

My intention in pointing out these contradictions is not to place blame on the students but to consider the pedagogical implications of the experience. For high school juniors encountering this sort of work for the first time, their answers were thoughtful and often impressive. The problem, I suggest, is that this project introduced a different and in some ways more complicated form of writing than is typical in the curriculum, raising new issues without adequately helping students to understand them. The confusion seems to have detracted from their appreciation of the value of argument, leaving them unclear about how writing with a point can be responsible and important and, more generally, about the role of perspective, narrative, and values in historical understanding.

This can fairly be seen as a shortcoming of the project. The students had been taught nothing about historiography, and we did not address argument during the project except in passing. For a teacher embarking on such a project, it would be advisable to bring these tensions to the surface and guide students in balanced consideration. The issues that students faced are perennial ones in the historical profession, as demonstrated by Novick's history of the "objectivity question," a staple of introductory doctoral seminars in history (1988). Tom's "just the facts" position calls to mind the empiricist directive, commonly associated with Leopold von Ranke, to portray the past "as it really was."[14] To give students more tools to reconcile the responsibility to evidence with other ethical commitments, this position could be contrasted with, say, an accessible statement of E. H. Carr's observation that historians necessarily choose what facts to study, even as they are responsive to them (1967).

I confess, though, that the issue remains a source of puzzlement for me. I wonder, for one thing, whether the similarity between WikiMarion and Wikipedia led students, quite reasonably, to think of their products as reference works. (The students did occasionally interchange the names of the two websites when speaking or typing web addresses.) To complicate matters further, some members of the public preferred the more reference-like articles, raising the possibility that there was more merit to the students' position than I have yet acknowledged. I take up this question in the next chapter. Not all of these issues are likely to be resolved in a high school history class, but even so, the students' comments suggest that this sort of project offers the chance to introduce them to an enduring intellectual dilemma, give them a sense of how to navigate it in their writing, and provoke questions for them to carry forward.

Conclusion

This was a complex project, and to the extent that students learned from it, the success might be attributed to multiple elements besides the fact that the students were working to create valuable products. First, the lynching is a uniquely compelling topic—an extreme case, as I have called it—and it was integral to the project; features of the subject matter are impossible to extricate from students' discussion of their work. Readers might reasonably wonder how a project would unfold with different subject matter or under otherwise different circumstances. It is my assumption—largely untested, although in previous chapters I have introduced a range of suggested project ideas—that there are other topics sufficiently interesting and meaningful to provide valuable learning experiences, if rarely to the same degree as this one. I return, in this book's conclusion, to the question of whether and how other fruitful projects might be created.

There are also points in this chapter at which the reader might wonder whether students' learning experiences should be attributed not to "value production" nor to the subject matter of the lynching in particular, but to the fact that the subject matter was local. It is true enough that one could imagine an instructional unit in which students were taught about local or community history without making their own contributions, and that this might have valuable consequences for their learning, regardless of whether their work products had a public audience. In the project I have described, however, there are good reasons at least to partially ascribe this "local" learning to the fact that students were learning through service. This sort of learning, as I have discussed it, involves contributing to audiences outside the school in ways that the students and audience members can potentially see as valuable. It could not take place without such an audience, and in the field of history, audiences like the ones addressed here—the Marion community, religious denominations, African American communities, a larger web-browsing public—seem like a good place to start. If, in the course of creating such value, students re-think their own positions in relation to those groups, it is reasonable to attribute this learning, in part, to the activity. Finally, by creating new texts—retelling the community's story, as Bellah and his colleagues (1985) put it—the students (and the historians, librarians, journalists, teachers, and playwrights) are contributing to a context of meaning in which further worthwhile work can take place. Readers are invited to consider other groups to which students might contribute, but it is impossible to imagine this sort of learning taking place in their absence.

In this chapter, I have examined the values perceived by students in their wiki projects on the lynching. Taken as a whole, I think, the weight of evidence points to a successful project that addressed many facets of understanding traditionally recognized as important in historical study, while also revealing an additional form of understanding that relates to the public values of history and the ways in which that history is made. However, these successes rest on the idea, yet unproved in the course of this book, that students can produce work of real value to members of the public. This is the question I take up in the next chapter.

· 5 ·

REALIZING THE PUBLIC VALUES OF LEARNING

Most of the students participating in this project, we can now say, saw their work as having value for themselves and others. Yet did others see the work as having such value? How would readers respond, and would they find value in the same places the students saw it? To answer these questions, I turned to the community, identifying audience members from a variety of backgrounds, presenting them with the students' wiki pages, and then soliciting their assessments of the pages' quality and the project's value. In the first half of this chapter, I discuss interviews with members of the public from various walks of life, most of them from the Marion community, including a newspaper editor, a prosecuting attorney, and two members of the library's local history staff. In the chapter's second half, I report on the reactions of four trained historians.

These interviews serve several purposes: They provide an external sense of the quality and value of the exhibit as seen from different points of view. The reviewers are critical in places, but their overall assessments are largely positive, establishing with reasonable confidence that the students made real contributions to public knowledge. They also show *how* a sampling of people read and evaluated the work—the grounds on which they judged its quality, the sorts of critiques and suggestions they made, and the types of value they saw. By identifying the various ways in which people evaluated the work—and in which the projects contributed to those readers' learning—we can better imagine and design new, worthwhile learning activities. By better understanding the criteria for judgment—topic selection, writing style, analysis, and others—we can help students hone their abilities to produce valuable work.

There is one further way in which these interviews can be interpreted: as a final phase of the project and the learning process. Although the interviews may at first appear to be a purely academic research method—a technique of inspection that stands apart from the project itself—they can also represent a model of learning for teachers and even, with some modifications, for students, as they would see how the community engages with their work. Chapter 1 suggests how the CHP has functioned as a form of professional development for Mr. Munn, helping to deepen his knowledge of Marion's history, historical research, and the ways in which history functions in society. This learning occurred, in part, as he built a network of community members and historians. In this chapter, having helped to teach this project myself, I return to some of these observers and add a few new ones, collecting their feedback in a more systematic way. They provide ideas for new topics, leads for sources, and distinctive types of feedback, all of which begin to suggest the range of resources that can be tapped within a community, especially regarding work of public consequence. A limited version of this process might even be incorporated into students' work, allowing them to meet their audience and gauge their reactions, completing a cycle of production, publication, feedback, and reflection.

Community members

The four historians who reviewed the project will be introduced and discussed later in the chapter. The seven community members, who were not historians, can be briefly introduced as follows:

- Rhonda Stoffer was the head of Indiana History and Genealogical Services at the Marion Public Library. She had worked with CHP students on several occasions, including during the lynching project. She had spent most of her lifetime living in Wells County, northeast of Marion.
- Martha Davis[1] was an employee of the Marion Public Library's Indiana Room and was knowledgeable about local history and the lynching. She had been employed at the library for more than a decade after retiring

from a career in retail management, and she had worked with students from the CHP on multiple occasions.

- Sylvia Williams was a homemaker in Marion and had lived in town her entire life. She had once worked as a child advocate, accompanying abused children to court, and was long involved at her children's schools in various capacities, tutoring, serving on textbook adoption committees, and running an after-school game room.
- Ed Breen, a resident of Marion since 1965, worked for many years at Marion's *Chronicle-Tribune*, holding "every job in the newsroom" on his way to the position of editor. For the final fifteen years of his career, he served as assistant managing editor of Fort Wayne's *Journal Gazette*. In semiretirement at the time of our interview, he was working part-time in local radio, serving as news analyst on the same morning show where Mr. Munn presented a weekly historical segment. Breen was active in the Indiana Historical Society and was a trustee of a significant Fort Wayne–based collection of Abraham Lincoln memorabilia. He was featured as a commentator in a documentary about the lynching produced by an Indianapolis PBS affiliate.
- Tim Eckerle was executive director of the Grant County Economic Growth Council, with an office on the courthouse square in downtown Marion. A native Chicagoan, he had lived in Marion for twenty-six years, all of them spent in his current position.
- James Luttrull was the elected prosecuting attorney for Indiana's Forty-Eighth Judicial Circuit, working from an office in the Grant County Courthouse. In that capacity, he was involved in the 2003 reconciliation efforts and issued an official statement of regret for the lynching. A Marion native and the son of an Indiana Wesleyan professor, he had left town for law school but returned home in 1983 and had practiced law there ever since.
- Becky Boyle was a social studies teacher in Bloomington, Indiana. She began teaching in 1988 and had taught high school economics, U.S. history and government, and seventh- and eighth-grade social studies. She had heard of the Marion lynching but had never met Mr. Munn and knew nothing of the CHP.

In these conversations, interviewees' responses to the project were strikingly reflective of their roles in the community—most often, their professional roles. For example, a former newspaper editor brought his editorial eye to the work, a librarian was especially attentive to library sources, and so forth. To best convey this quality of the responses, discussion in this chapter is organized by the interviewees' roles, with occasional interruptions to show cross-cutting themes.

Rhonda Stoffer and Martha Davis—Library local history staff

As employees of the public library's Indiana Room, Rhonda Stoffer and Martha Davis were among the interviewees most familiar with Marion's history and its documentary record. This local knowledge, displayed throughout their comments, was particularly evident as Stoffer examined Jennifer's WikiMarion page on Marion in the 1920s. Stoffer was generally pleased with the way Jennifer offered context for the lynching, but she noticed that a postcard of the courthouse square appeared to be misdated. The postcard was said to be from the 1930s, but the trees in the image were too short. The postcard, she concluded, should be dated earlier. This mistake is rendered particularly significant by the role of those trees in the lynching story, but the dating of images is a specialty of these local historians, and the knowledge they draw upon, of everything from clothing to car models, has been accumulated over a lifetime. Similarly, Martha Davis was able to contextualize and thereby complicate one student's implication that Sheriff Campbell could have used more than tear gas when trying to disperse the assembling mob. Davis basically agreed with the student's judgment, but she pointed out that the police at that time lacked rubber bullets and Tasers, so his options were limited. Stoffer's and Davis's depth of knowledge would be impossible to impart quickly to students, and other educational goals should probably take priority, but it is useful for the teacher to know of community members who can alert students to possible problems and model more accomplished analysis. (It is a shortcoming of the process that the students did not receive this feedback directly, because the interviews were carried out several months after the project's end. Note, however, that many did receive similar guidance from Davis and Stoffer during visits to the Indiana Room.)

Small mistakes aside, Stoffer was pleased with the work and said she would be comfortable recommending it to library patrons seeking information. She and another librarian had driven to Indianapolis to see *The Gospel According to James*, and Stoffer judged that Hannah and Carmen had represented it faithfully. Hannah had quoted from online reviews, and Stoffer noted that she had chosen phrases that effectively captured the experience. She also found Eric's guide to lynching resources to be helpful in the way it "abstracted" other information sources, and she was gratified to see the library first on his list. As in Becky Boyle's comments on the value of collection and curation, below, Stoffer draws attention to the service provided as students condense, review, and filter information. These are important functions in the flow of knowledge and culture, seen everywhere from scholarly peer review, to film criticism, to social media linking. Moreover, the skills required are important ones, ranging from summarization to critical judgment.

Like Rhonda Stoffer, Martha Davis was complimentary of the overall exhibit, calling it "very well done." Reading Emily's page, she said, "This is giving more than I had ever heard about Mary Ball." Having read virtually every available source, Davis was in a position to make this statement, and she correctly singled out the discoveries about Ball's California life as Emily's most original contribution. Davis also liked Lynn's page on newspaper coverage of the lynching, saying she had appropriately interpreted a political cartoon and had selected articles from different newspapers, including black newspapers such as the *Chicago Defender*, which effectively illustrated their varied editorial viewpoints. "I think she's done a really good job, because she is showing the difference between the two points of view—from Marion's point of view… and then from the outside world," Davis said. Comparing this project with a traditional term paper, she thought the experience of archival research would be constructive: "I would say this would be much more valuable to them than just being able to go on the Internet and pull off different articles…. I'm not talking about the subject matter. What I'm speaking of is being able to do research, and to document that research and then to come up with their own opinions of things." This statement resonates with several of the students' own self-assessments cited in Chapter 4; indeed, it is possible that Davis employed this language while working with students and thereby shaped their interpretation of the work.

One criticism from this pair of interviews, though not strongly worded, strikes me as especially noteworthy. I showed both women Michael's biographical page on Thomas Shipp, which he had researched in the Indiana Room. Each recognized that Michael was relying heavily on James Cameron's version of events, even where skepticism was in order. Describing the initial alleged stickup, Michael writes, "Shipp and Smith both suggested robbing someone for some extra money, but Cameron insisted he was not interested. Shipp and Smith ignored his request." In Michael's telling, the boys then set off to

Lover's Lane and advanced on the car that belonged to Mary Ball and Claude Deeter, the latter of whom was Cameron's shoeshine client and friend. "When Cameron realized it was Deeter, he gave the gun back to Shipp and ran off," wrote Michael, "leaving the others to finish the crime." The account clearly serves to exonerate Cameron, and although there is no particular reason to suspect him as the triggerman, the story cries out for a critical reading. Stoffer quickly inferred the source of this story, saying that the piece seemed "a little more swayed to Cameron's version." Cameron's story should be included, she said, but she would have preferred a more "neutral" treatment like Madison's on WikiMarion. I find this criticism—as well as Davis's similar comments—to be entirely fair. The project was no silver bullet for teaching historical reasoning. If there is any consolation, it is at least encouraging that Stoffer and Davis were able to provide this feedback, based on their knowledge of events and not special historical training. A skilled teacher might identify this as an opportunity for learning.

Sylvia Williams—Homemaker and child advocate

As I have said, I encouraged readers to provide assessments of students' work, but it often seemed that their more natural impulse was to use the work as a point of departure for their own stories and reflections on race in Marion. This was especially true of my conversation with Sylvia Williams, a middle-aged African American woman. When specifically prompted for evaluation, Williams expressed approval and gratitude, but she invariably returned to storytelling or reflection. We looked last at Carmen and Hannah's page on *The Gospel According to James*, and Sylvia's response here was typical. "They did a good job on it," she said, and asked whether she could keep the printouts to read after I had gone. (This interview was conducted using a paper version of the project because of limited Internet access.) "They taught me things I didn't even know. When it talked about... the cutting and the different things, I never knew that part." But with this chilling thought, she immediately shifted back to a mode of somber meditation: "What I always say, too, [is,] 'Everybody is somebody's child.' What about the parents? Can you imagine the hurt they felt?" It is clear that Williams was learning new information from the project, but equally clear was the empathy she brought to it.

Among many memories, Mrs. Williams told of her childhood walks to Horace Mann Elementary School, which took her directly past the lynching tree. "I was always afraid of that side of the street," she said. "Sometimes, people don't realize a child pays attention, or what that does to a child, but there was always that fear of that tree and also the courthouse." She would make a path around the block to avoid the tree, which, she speculated, had been "left there to say, 'Stay in your place.'" Thinking then of the present day, Williams lamented the high incarceration rates of young African American men and expressed fear on behalf of her three grandsons, one of whom played on the floor nearby. As an interviewer, this was the most personally affecting moment of my conversations with community members, and it made me especially aware that my job was not only to ask questions but also to listen sympathetically and to share in moments of strong emotion. There is no doubt that Williams appreciated many aspects of the students' work, but this moment above all helped me to appreciate most viscerally how the value of the work is realized through the experiences to which it gives rise.

Ed Breen—Newspaper editor

While working at the *Chronicle-Tribune*, Ed Breen had edited stories on the lynching, and he was keen to talk about sources that went untapped in the students' work, especially a reporter with whom he had worked in the mid-1970s. The reporter, he recollected, had interviewed both James Cameron and Mary Ball, and Breen thought a student might consult his articles or speak with him directly. He also suggested making a page on Cameron's 1993 pardon and conducting an interview with James Madison about how his research was carried out. Breen initially questioned the pertinence of two pages, including Tom's treatment of previous criminal activity in the neighborhood of Lovers' Lane. He ultimately relaxed these judgments, given that the website placed no limitations on space, but he felt that there were more important topics to be covered. These sorts of comments—identifying neglected sources or topics—were relatively frequent among local interviewees. Martha Davis felt there should be a page on Jack Edwards, mayor at the time of the lynching. Tim Eckerle questioned the lack of articles on Abram Smith and Claude Deeter. Similar comments were made by historians who lived in the area. These are helpful suggestions, and they seem especially apt to come from knowledgeable locals, who could profitably be consulted at the beginning of the project and not only at the end.

Breen initially expressed chagrin that Emily had repeated certain salacious details regarding Mary Ball that had previously been published in other sources. Breen preferred restraint in printing what he regarded as gossip, but after weighing both sides of the matter, he decided that his quarrel was not with Emily, and that she was justified in including the information. "This is well done and complete and probably needs to be in the record," he said of the page. "The sourcing is good on it as far as I can tell. This isn't just pulled out of the sky." A journalist would likely apply standards of "sourcing" different from a historian's, but it is helpful to know that even in a small town, newspaper employees might be well acquainted with the documentary record and could be called upon to stress the importance of reading it critically. Breen noted a few problems with writing—*hung* instead of *hanged*, for instance, which he called a "copy editor's nit-pick." Across interviews, there were occasional mentions of writing problems or typos, but Breen and the Marion community members judged the site by and large to be well written. (Recall that I had contributed to this, marking some students' drafts in hard copy).

This quality, among others, factored into Breen's assessment of the project as a whole: "It's a sum of an enormous amount of material. It's been well edited, well presented. It's there for anybody... as long as the Internet is around. It's going to be able to provide people with a very detailed look at a very important piece of Marion history." When I asked for potential downsides of the public aspect of the project, he told me I had come to the wrong person; as a newspaperman, providing access to information was one of his strongest personal commitments. "I would see a downside if I thought the thing were done in a slipshod way or was grossly inaccurate," he said, "But that's not the case." Breen judged that doing original research, with newspapers and other sources, "serves the students better" than a traditional term paper. He guessed that the students "came away from this with a feeling of having, first of all, learned something, been challenged, in a way that they hadn't been challenged before" and, secondly, of having done "something that had lasting merit." In contrast, he said, thinking back on his own education, "None of us ever wrote a term paper that we believed had a life of more than an hour and a half."

James Luttrull—Prosecuting attorney

James Luttrull maintained a standing interest in the lynching. As prosecutor, he had been invited to participate in the 2003 reconciliation events, and while he found it inappropriate to apologize per se for something that had happened many years before his birth, he issued a heartfelt and well-received statement of regret. He had also looked, unsuccessfully, for court records from the trials of alleged mob members and had read the surviving depositions from the Court of Inquiry investigation, which David had analyzed. Luttrull strongly approved of David's work, saying that the choice of quotations was "very appropriate," and that he, like David, found the evasions "hard to swallow." Luttrull was curious about the sources used and was pleased to find them specified in references at the bottom of the page. He did raise several technical legal questions, wondering, for example, whether David's use of the word "conspiracy" meant there was evidence of "a specific act of conspiracy or overt manipulation" or whether the cover-up was simply "in the atmosphere," as he had often seen in his work. I suspect David, as an aspiring attorney, would have relished this sort of discussion.

Luttrull was most moved by Samantha's page on "Strange Fruit" and by watching the YouTube video of the song she had embedded in the page. Luttrull liked Billie Holiday, he told me, but was unfamiliar with this song or its connection to the Marion lynching: "This is probably as fascinating as any page I've seen just because it's new information for me, and just having the link to the song gives it another dimension." Numerous interviewees appreciated this multimedia aspect of the project.[2] Like many interviewees, Luttrull appreciated the "accessibility" of the work. With a typical student paper, he said, "I'm never going to see it unless they're my next-door neighbor or my own kid. Even if it were filed somewhere at the public library, I wouldn't know it. But I could either stumble onto this [website] or intentionally go out and purposefully find it. So being accessible is... a big deal to me." I heard this sort of praise repeated many times. Over the years, Rhonda Stoffer of the Indiana Room had spent many hours putting student projects on file and into the card catalogue, but mostly, she said, they "sit on the shelf," unused. "If you can't come here [physically], it's not going to do any good for you." With the resources posted online instead, she said, people can read from "wherever they are in the world." This increased accessibility, she judged, was a "big benefit."

Though not a teacher, Luttrull made several acute points about the project's pedagogical strengths. Examining the work and making inferences about the process through which it was produced, Luttrul said that the project "could not have easily been done in a rush job, cramming the night before," a point my observations largely confirm. Luttrull also counted the "group aspect" of the wiki as a mark in the project's favor. He supposed that students would derive a feeling of shared responsibility by seeing the interdependence between each web page—the way "a weak page may weaken the overall project; a strong page strengthens it." This, he reckoned, would heighten each student's sense that they are "making a contribution and making a difference." Based on my observations, he probably overestimates the students' sense of shared purpose. This was more an individual than a group project. But the mutual assistance among classmates increased in the closing days of the project, and this aspect could perhaps be accentuated with more group discussions or joint products.

Tim Eckerle—Economic development director

Most interviewees were complimentary of the project, but one, economic development director Tim Eckerle, gave the project mixed grades. Asked for an overarching assessment, he said, noncommittally, "It's a range of eighteen students... of varying degrees of interest, of time, and skills." If anything, his comments were more negative than positive. He caught one outright error, a mistaken location of a factory, but if there was a general theme to his criticisms, it was that the students' bias showed in their work. Reading David's page on the legal treatment of suspected mob members, Eckerle said, "It's clear [the author has] a point of view that's come across.... It's not a factual piece. It's an argumentative piece. It's an opinionated piece." He drew attention to what he considered to be loaded word choices, like "gruesome" to describe the lynching and "manipulated" in reference to the legal proceedings. David had provided quotations from three of thirty depositions, asserting that the pattern of evasion and denial was repeated across the rest, but given David's obvious point of view, Eckerle was not prepared to trust these selections as representative. Eckerle's criticisms seemed, at least in part, to reflect preferences and assumptions that he brought to the project. He explained, "I don't look for opinion [in history articles] just like I don't look for opinion in my news articles. I'm looking for a factual representation." He made a similar criticism of another student project and even of Professor Madison's book on the lynching, which he had read previously. "I thought that he predetermined a single cause," said Eckerle—that "it was totally racially motivated." If James Luttrull is correct, David fairly represents the testimony, and his word choices cited above do not strike me as objectionable, but David did explain how he attempted to incorporate some emotion into the writing. It is possible that Eckerle would have been satisfied by a more distanced tone, but this would have displeased other readers who counted a well-supported argument as a positive good, and it would have undermined David's intention to convey the emotional tenor of the event.

I interviewed Eckerle in part because I had heard Marionites argue that continued attention to the lynching would drive away prospective businesses. My intention was to test this claim with someone positioned to know. Eckerle was indifferent, maintaining that the ramifications of the project would be mostly internal to Marion with little effect on business attraction. Over many years of work, he said, not once had he been asked about the lynching. The more salient issue was standardized test scores. Given the poor performance of local schools on these measures, he had resorted to selling the district with stories and materials that went "beyond the numbers." In this vein, he said, WikiMarion should be used in the district's "marketing," because it would reflect well on the schools and show an orientation toward "scholarship and academic achievement."

Eckerle saw learning potential in the project, believing that the local subject matter would be motivating for students, that the project would teach research and writing skills, and that, unlike a traditional paper, it could make an original contribution to the community, becoming a "point of reference" that people could "incorporate in future works." Because of these public consequences, he suggested that the project merited more class time, perhaps being worked on during "an entire year," so that it might reach a more consistent standard of quality. But on this count, he gave mixed messages, also saying that standardized test scores are the one school-related factor that relocating businesses consider and that the district should focus on meeting content standards, "no matter how superficial the content standards are."

Becky Boyle—Social studies teacher

Becky Boyle, an Indiana native who had heard of the Marion lynching but knew few details about it, brought a teacher's eye to the project. She considered the exhibit first as a resource for her own eighth-grade students and judged that most pages were well written at a level they would be able to understand. She did find a few problems in the students' writing: The vocabulary in one page seemed too complicated for her students, and she faulted another for short sentences without sufficient detail. But all things considered, Boyle said that if she were teaching in Marion, she "wouldn't hesitate" to point her students to the site as a source for their research and added that it would provide resources she could use to "hook" students on project ideas for National

History Day. Boyle's judgments here are pertinent, given that younger students form an obvious audience for the work. High school juniors are not far removed from the experience of eighth grade, and it is no leap to think that they could imagine their audience members as younger versions of themselves. What is more, they seem to find this kind of audience meaningful; one thinks of Carmen sharing her project with a younger brother and Tom's interest in teaching the "next generation." It was encouraging, then, to hear that the exchange might be profitable for their younger counterparts as well.

Later in the interview, considering students as producers of local history rather than consumers, Boyle was enthusiastic about the project's engagement potential. As a teacher, she said, she spent a great deal of time trying to answer the question "Why is learning this important?" and to help students "to make... connections to something bigger, [so] that it's not just the topic." The meaning of the last phrase remains slightly ambiguous, but reading it in light of my experience in Mr. Munn's class and others, I take Boyle to be saying that the project conveys aspects of history's importance that go beyond the intrinsic significance of any given event. She had conducted oral history projects in which students interviewed military veterans and found that the students were "touched," "hooked," and "changed by talking to people about their experiences"—to such an extent that they would refer to the conversations months later.

One final comment from Becky Boyle brings into sharper focus a form of value that has been only implicit in the discussion to this point. Looking at WikiMarion, Boyle was reminded of local history research carried out at a Bloomington high school. That project, she said admiringly, creates new resources and makes them accessible—by now a familiar refrain. But more than that, it "pulls... other resources together in a collection under a specific topic that was never created or designed that way before." All of this she called "incredibly valuable." Boyle's comments call attention to a sort of curatorial value that becomes more viable once an initiative like the CHP has generated sufficient artifacts to be re-assembled and re-interpreted in light of new themes, arguments, or narratives.

Discussion

In the interviews summarized above, student projects were given generally positive marks. Six of the interviewees, although they made occasional criticisms, gave the work a clear show of approval. The seventh, Tim Eckerle, offered a mixed review, leaning negative. These interviews do not allow for a definitive tallying of value, but they do provide encouraging signs that students can do worthwhile work, and, in fact, they show value being realized as the community members read. It is apparent that several of the interviewees learned through the process and that most found the projects quite interesting—even engrossing. The encounters were also sources of learning for me, and if incorporated more fully into the project, they might advance the learning of students as well. The community members brought relevant knowledge to the reading, were able to identify mistakes and suggest further projects and resources, and demonstrated capacities to make critical judgments that would have helped students to revise their work. Finally, the projects and the task of evaluation prompted meaningful encounters between me and the interviewees—occasions for telling stories, sharing memories, building relationships, and advancing mutual understanding.

The interviewees' grounds for judgment included the selection of topics, the quality and tone of writing, the inclusion of interactive multimedia resources, the degree to which projects provided readers with context, the selection of historical sources, and the quality of analysis. Like the students, they placed great stock in the importance of providing access to information as well as in the creation, preservation, and interpretation of artifacts. Most of the interviewees seemed to presume that learning had taken place in a variety of ways. Some saw signs that it had sparked students' interest, imparted knowledge about an important local event, and introduced them to new skills of research, writing, and analysis. The community member comments also go beyond what students were able to say, pointing to new functions such as collection, curation, and review.

One point from these interviews, not yet mentioned, should give pause. Both members of the library staff, Rhonda Stoffer and Martha Davis, mentioned independently that the quality of this work was higher than they had seen in recent years. Stoffer waxed nostalgic about the early days of the project, when they had double-staffed the library and rearranged their Sunday hours to accommodate the class's needs. "It was tiring, but it was fun," she recalled. But they had been called upon less frequently as time passed, and the quality of projects and particularly the quality of writing had declined. There are a number of possible explanations. I suspect that some of the initial novelty of the work had worn off, and that evening library hours proved difficult for Mr. Munn to sustain as he moved toward retirement. With pressure to cover historical content and no English teacher to partner with on writing issues, less time had been spent on revision. The educational context also presented obstacles, among them regional socioeconomic decline, low test scores, a school-wide probationary label, and a culture that was increasingly test driven with less time for project-based learning. Likewise, the success in spring 2011 likely owed to the urgency of the subject matter and the help I was able to provide. Quality and enthusiasm, Mr. Munn judged, were up across the board, even among his other students who were not research subjects. This caveat need not invalidate the experiences I describe in these pages. The students' investment and learning were no less powerful, and some of the challenges might be mitigated by future research and design. Digitization of newspapers and other sources could soon bring the archives into the classroom, and videoconferencing could bring the archivists alongside. Some teachers will find it easier to partner with English teachers, and historical writing may take on greater importance in new sets of curriculum standards. But Stoffer and Davis did sound a cautionary note about the sustainability of the project within the current educational environment, and their comments should temper expectations about the practicality of replication in its current form.

Historians

Many of the above interviews were conducted with community members highly knowledgeable about the lynching, but for a different kind of expertise, I turned to four historians. All held doctorates in the field, though not all were actively publishing—one had become a full-time parish priest. All had also been college-level teachers of history as well as scholars, and so, having spent time reading student work and reflecting on historical learning, they were well positioned to evaluate the wiki projects and comment on their apparent pedagogical strengths and limitations.

I hoped that the historians would bring to bear concerns informed by their disciplinary traditions, but to be clear, it would be a mistake to view student articles as potentially perfectible as works of history. It would be unreasonable to hold them to the standards of the professional historian, and though I did not provide any explicit instructions on this point, the historians seemed generally inclined to take students' age into account when evaluating the work. Still, what the historians can tell us is whether, under these circumstances, students at an intermediate stage of development can do worthwhile public historical work and whether this sort of project provides opportunities for teachers to take stock of students' understanding of the event itself, as well as the discipline of history, and to work with them to advance that understanding. As it happens, their answer for both questions is yes. Accounting for both strengths and shortcomings, they judged the projects to be worthwhile, contributing to the students' historical understandings and providing Marion with an important resource. At the same time, their comments point to ways in which the work could be improved and student understandings deepened.

As with many of the interviewees, several of the historians had existing relationships with Bill Munn, and in fact Munn had actually met two of them through his public history initiatives. Thus, I was returning to them and asking that they examine CHP student work more systematically than they had previously done. The historians are as follows:

- James Madison, author of the definitive book on the Marion lynching (2001), had recently retired from Indiana University's history department, where he had earned his doctorate and later served as department chair. All told, he had written six scholarly books relating to Indiana including a comprehensive state history, *The Indiana Way* (1986). Madison had met Munn while conducting research for his lynching book in the mid-1990s and had written letters in support of early CHP grant applications.
- Jerry Pattengale held a Ph.D. in history from Miami University of Ohio. When we spoke, he was serving as assistant provost and professor of ancient history at Marion's Indiana Wesleyan University. Pattengale had witnessed the CHP in action, as students restored the Weaver Cemetery near his rural home south of Marion, and although he and Munn did not work closely together, he had since written in support.[3]
- James Warnock had earned a doctorate in history from the University of Washington with a focus on late nineteenth-century American religion and intellectual history. He had taught for several years at the college level before becoming an Episcopal priest. At the time of the interview, he served a parish in Marion and continued to teach U.S. history survey classes as an adjunct professor at nearby Taylor University. Warnock's son had once been a student in Munn's class, carrying out two local history projects, and Munn was a member of Warnock's congregation.
- Russell 'Rusty' Hawkins had recently earned his Ph.D. in history from Rice University with a focus on race and Christianity in the American South. When we spoke, he was a postdoctoral fellow at Indiana Wesleyan

University, where he is now, as of this writing, an associate professor. Hawkins was a newcomer to the area and had not met Bill Munn, giving him more distance from the project than other interviewees.

Historians' evaluations

Each of the four historians was moderately pleased by the quality of student work. In Warnock's judgment, the papers ranged from "really, really good to just good." Madison said that he hadn't seen anything "brilliant," at least in the projects he reviewed, and that there were places where writing was "mediocre," but that in general, "for high school kids... it's a very high quality." Of the four historians, Hawkins was probably the most critical, as detailed below, but in the final analysis, he said it was "incredible" to have done so much in such a short time. Near the end of our interview, asked to compare the wiki projects with term papers, Hawkins said, "Two months... of those students working on this and you're able to cover that [many] different perspectives and different sides of the issue, and then have all that information available for public consumption. Certainly it outpaces the paper assignment."

In some cases, the historians' comments mirrored those heard from other members of the community, adding weight to those judgments but providing little in the way of additional insight. (They were, after all, reviewing the same projects, many of which had obvious strengths and weaknesses.) I begin by reviewing a few of these briefly, providing supporting evidence in footnotes to minimize repetition: Three historians mentioned the appeal of multimedia, typically taking a teacher's or author's perspective and noting that photographs, maps, and videos would hold the attention of both students and viewers.[4] One historian, Madison, joined librarian Rhonda Stoffer in praising a project for providing helpful historical context, which he said was vital to understanding the lynching and its significance. The historians were perhaps slightly more critical of student writing than were the other community members. Each of the four noted specific errors, from missing italics to a "muddled" thesis statement, but two also praised student writing at other points, and none regarded the writing issues as particularly surprising or worrisome.[5]

Like librarian Martha Davis, both Madison and Hawkins praised the diversity of perspectives and topics covered. Hawkins appreciated that the exhibit showed "many different sides to a story," giving "a three-dimensional complexity to something that students would otherwise see as, kind of, two-dimensional, flat." Indeed, as seen in the previous chapter, some students did remark on an increased sense of historical complexity. In one case, a historian pointed out a missing perspective: James Warnock was largely impressed by Ashley's treatment of the reconciliation events—he had participated in them as a clergyman and said that her account rang true—but he noted an absence of African American voices. In particular, Rev. Larry Batchelor had been very involved, and Warnock called the failure to mention him an "obvious omission." (I pointed out that another student, Munn's son Alex, had spoken with Batchelor and mentioned him on a different wiki page, but Warnock held firm, insisting that his perspective should have been included in both places.)

As with members of the general public, the task of evaluation at times receded, and the historians read to satisfy personal interests. All four noted moments when they were learning new things: Warnock remarked that he was learning things about the reconciliation events that he had not previously known, and Pattengale said the same about the Beitler photograph. Having written at length about the lynching, Madison had less to learn, but even he saw a photograph of Mary Ball with which he was unfamiliar. Hawkins, new to town and with the least background knowledge, became most absorbed. This is evident in the interview transcript as he read aloud the closing of the Klan's letter to Carol Secttor, "How fascinating. 'For God, country and race. Grant County Klan #10.' Holy cow, it's 1970," he said, surprised to see this sort of Klan activity at so late a date. Later in the interview, having seen more interesting links than we had time to explore, Hawkins volunteered, "I want to go back to visit sometime on my own time"—strong testimony to the work's appeal.

Drawing on their experiences as college-level teachers, the historians commented at length about the project's likely consequences for students' individual learning. In this respect, there was universal agreement that the project was valuable, on grounds that it would both provoke a greater-than-usual intensity of engagement and promote types of understanding difficult to achieve by other means. One reason for the perceived engagement gains involved the immediacy of both oral history interviews and primary sources. Warnock, having assigned oral histories as a college teacher and witnessed one firsthand as the parent of a CHP student, observed that these projects often involve powerfully direct moments of interpersonal connection. Warnock's own son had interviewed his grandfather—Warnock's father-in-law—about his experiences in World War II. The grandfather, who was Jewish, had been among the American soldiers to open German concentration camps. He had not previously talked about those experiences but opened up to Warnock's son—an affecting experience for all involved. Reading Jason's interview with his grandmother, Warnock pictured a similar sort of encounter, which Jason's own reflections confirm. Hawkins was similarly effusive about the directness and power of primary sources. Examining scanned copies of the Klan letter and pamphlets, he noted their tactile quality and the way in which reading a handwritten note gave the feeling of unmediated connection across time. Students, he hoped, would be "somewhat shocked" to see this kind of evidence of Klan activity, as well they were. The documents' physical texture, which comes across in the digital scans Hawkins viewed, was surely even more noticeable as students passed them around a table.

Professor Madison's comments were the most developed in connecting engagement, civic action, and the nature of historical understanding. He thought students would approach this differently from a normal project, and for several specific reasons: the multimedia product, the public audience, and the connection of both the subject matter and the learning activity to the local community. These would, together, intensify students' experience of the project, making them more "intellectually... and emotionally connected to the subject," with a "sense that the stakes here are a little higher." He saw this as "higher level learning" that, when compared with traditional classwork, would be "more likely to have consequences after the assignment is finished."

When I asked what those consequences might be, Madison cited the way in which the project would make the past seem real. Drawing on a career of teaching and public engagement, he had already explained what he saw as one challenge of history education, saying, with a rhetorical flourish, "I have this sense that young Americans don't really believe there was a past.... No one came before them, despite what their history books tell." In light of this present-mindedness, the history teacher must find ways "to convince students that there really was a past. There really were live human beings who lived lives different from and similar to yours." Oral histories and primary documents, said Madison, are especially useful tools to that end, far more likely than a term paper to convince students "that race worked in different ways in the 1920s than it does in 2010—that African Americans and white Americans lived differently in their relationship to each other in Marion, Indiana, in 1930 before the lynching." (For one thing, as his book explains, there had been a burgeoning black middle class that, in the absence of lynching, might have developed very differently.) Of course, these encounters with history can also bring home the reality of the oppressive order that set in. Alluding to Jason's interview with his grandmother, Madison said, "Talking to someone who can tell this young man directly that she remembers sitting in the segregated part of the theater—that probably is as important in terms of understanding segregation as the Montgomery Bus Boycott, reading about that in the textbook."

In Madison's view, helping students grasp the reality of the past was ultimately a way of instilling a sense of belonging to and taking responsibility for a community. By participating in the project, he hoped, students would "begin to feel that they are citizens of this community. That they have a stake in this community. That what happened before is important to their citizenship in that community and that it gives them obligations to the community down the road." Based on the work he had seen, he said, "For some of these students, that's a likely outcome." One can imagine a number of ways in which students might develop this sense of investment and obligation. They might first, like Zachary, feel themselves compelled by a story that "needs to be told." By telling that story, they might, like Ashley, come to appreciate Marion as community and not just a mailing address. In the course of their work, they might strengthen ties to other people and institutions in the community or rethink their own identity in light of the community story. Having contributed to it—having taken a "stake" in the community—they might be more likely to carry that work forward, as I myself have done.

The historians' overall reaction, then, was positive, and all four saw a place for public work in the history curriculum. When I asked them to compare the wiki projects with the students' first-semester papers, however, each also saw some relative advantages for the traditional term paper. Hawkins put it pointedly, saying that the traditional term paper is "a good exercise in sustained reasoning,... the ability to carry through on an argument longer than a paragraph." The wiki format, he said, is more conducive to "short snippets" than "sustained argumentation." Again, this is confirmed by some of the students' comments, like Tom's sense that he was writing without "trying to get a point across." Pattengale agreed, saying that in web projects, students "are not forced to develop a thesis." If a project fails to give students "the ability to articulate hypotheses and conclusions and [reason from] premise-premise-to-entailment, then I think that you've developed a chronicler but not a thinker." For Pattengale, these statements were wrapped up in broader epistemological concerns. He expressed some trepidation that Wikipedia might lead to the "democratization of truth," which he opposed (though he was satisfied that WikiMarion, which does not allow outside editing, is not especially problematic in that regard). Pattengale twice referenced the medieval text *Sic et Non*, in which the theologian Abelard takes up five perennial questions of Christian theology and presents quotations from church fathers arguing both sides of every issue. For Pattengale, this style of thought was to be avoided. Rather than contemplating that the answer could be both yes and no, or that truth might emerge from the dialectic between the two, students should be taught to take a position and defend it tenaciously.

Pattengale's positions are not my own, but I have acknowledged in Chapter 4 that the lack of argumentation can be seen as a limitation of some students' work and merits greater attention. Teachers might address the issue more deliberately or guide students toward other written genres, such as blog entries or long-form articles, that are better suited to argument. *The Concord Review*, which has published student-written journal articles since 1987, offers another model in this vein (Dillon, 2011). During these eleven interviews, however, I was struck by most participants' reluctance to actually read the sustained arguments that some students had produced, such as Alex's essay on memorialization and accountability. They seemed more inclined to scan a page, occasionally alighting on certain passages for closer reading. Perhaps this reflects, in part, the time-limited format of the interview, but it also agrees with conventional wisdom about the way people read web pages.[6] Is it possible that the students who wrote reference-style texts, with headings and discrete sections, had best understood the constraints of the medium or the appetites of their audience? Notwithstanding its traditional importance in the history classroom, argumentation is only one among many modes of historical exposition, and some contexts call for different ones—narrative, analysis, even reference. Teaching students to argue about historical matters using historians' techniques is an important goal, but when a situation calls for students to operate in other modes, this objection should not hold sway.

The observations above show historians reflecting on pedagogical affordances and limitations of wikis and public projects in general, but they also, occasionally, posed critiques of the particular arguments that they read. One pattern of comments concerning students' ways of explaining the relationship between racism, the Klan, and the lynching shows how historians' feedback might be useful in pushing students toward increasingly sophisticated arguments and understandings. To begin with, Warnock noted an analytical error in the following passage from Ben's page on Sheriff Jake

Campbell, who is often criticized for a failure to secure the jail against the lynch mob:

> Campbell was said to possibly have ties with the notorious Ku Klux Klan (Madison 36–63). It was not uncommon at this time for a sheriff or person with higher power to have direct ties to the Klan ("Muncie Evening Press" Page 1). Although Jake was never proven to be a Klan member it seems to make sense that he would be, because of his lack of protection for the three young African American men.

Reading these last words aloud, Warnock demurred: "That actually doesn't necessarily follow. There could be a lot of other reasons. Maybe he was afraid of the Klan, wasn't a member but he's afraid to act." Ben himself made this same point later in the paragraph, which partially satisfied Warnock, though he remained justifiably critical of the presentation.

I had noticed this problem myself as Ben was working on the project, and I made a comment on one of his drafts, but the problem went unresolved. Initially, I regarded the mistake as a simple error in reasoning. But upon further consideration, I have come to see it as at least suggestive of a deeper and apparently widely held misunderstanding. There is a tentativeness in Ben's statement—"it seems to make sense" that Campbell would have been a Klan member—but the reasoning is backward in a way that suggests an assumption that the Klan was the primary locus of racial animus and perhaps even its source: If a person is racist, it stands to reason that he is a Klan member or, at the very least, has fallen under its influence. Insufficient consideration is given to the reality that racism existed far beyond and independent of the Klan. Madison frequently speaks about the tendency among contemporary readers to lay the lynching at the Klan's feet, when in fact it can be conclusively stated that the Klan was not involved. The group had played a major role in Indiana in the 1920s, its influence peaking with the election of Grand Dragon D. C. Stephenson as governor in 1924. But after Stephenson was convicted of the abduction and rape of his secretary in 1925, membership cratered. This left the state with many *former* Klan members, and Sheriff Campbell may have been one, but the organization had all but disappeared—and racism, injustice, and persecution, of course, both pre- and post-dated its heyday.

For Rusty Hawkins, this sort of faulty attribution was weighty with moral significance. Having come across several mentions of the Klan in various student wiki pages, he noted that this seemed like a way of confining responsibility for the lynching to an easy scapegoat:

> It almost seems as if undue influence gets given to the Ku Klux Klan in all this. As if students are looking for a way to explain this that goes beyond latent racism that resides in all of us, or something like that. It's almost as if students are desperately trying to link this to the Klan for the purpose of explaining it away. Like, how much easier it is to say, yes it was the Klan rather than to deal with the fact that there are other factors driving these things.

If blame can be pinned on a single group that has long since been relegated to the fringes of society, then responsibility can be evaded with little examination of one's own culture and self and with little consideration of contributing causes that might still be at work. I was aware of this danger before the project began and took steps to avoid it (hence the decision to post Carol Secttor's Klan documents in a section of WikiMarion separate from the lynching project), but it is difficult to contest Hawkins's observation that it appears to some extent in the finished product.

Madison made a similar comment, discussing a passage in which a student called newspaper coverage "blatantly racist"—accurately, but in a way that may have simplified and dismissed the issue much as a Klan reference can: "Students in my university classes, and I think in high school history classes, they want those kind of labels that seem to provide the explanation, and the teacher then has to find ways to move them beyond that—toward a more subtle, ambiguous kind of history." For many students, the project did seem to convey an enhanced sense of complexity and ambiguity, but these excerpts show the limits of that progress. I have previously suggested, based on my conversations with students, that the focus of this project on creation of public artifacts may have worked against a certain kind of deeper understanding, limiting, as it did, the time available for reflection and discussion. What is notable about Madison's and Hawkins's comments is, first, that they arrived at similar conclusions through a close analysis of students' written work, and, second, that their critiques gesture toward ways of deepening students' understanding that might emerge from the process of improving their texts. The implication is that reflection and production are not necessarily at odds, and that reflection in this sort of project might be grounded in the process of critique and revision.

One final point of criticism shows a student with similar misapprehensions and an opportunity for increased historical sophistication. Ashley's paper, as we have seen, explored the relationship between the church and the lynching. In the paper, she quotes an ominous question, posed by a pastor involved in the reconciliation events, and then begins to answer it:

> "You can not help but ask yourself the question, 'Where were the white Christians when they were hanging those two black boys?'" said Rev. Mike Henson, pastor of Bethel Worship Center, to the members of the Grant County Ethnic Diversity Task Force on Tuesday, October 7, 2003. "I ask myself that question. Where were they?" ("Family Protests Plaque")
>
> The "white Christians" were likely in the crowd. Possibly at home, either unaware or unattached from the scene of the crime, but evidence indicates that many church-goers had taken a part in the Marion Lynching.

I asked Hawkins to examine this article, given its proximity to his own research interests, and he read, past this passage, to the following lines in which Ashley qualifies that statement: "Note, however, that the beliefs held by the Klan were not held by the actual church, but of people in the church. Christians had also been very involved in abolition, Quakers especially, such as in the Underground Railroad." Hawkins fixed on the first sentence, which he took as an attempt to absolve the church of some responsibility: "That's a statement that historians wouldn't make. As a Christian myself, I can make this claim. I wouldn't make that claim as a historian because, what is a church if not what people believe, right?" Ashley returned to the point in the conclusion of her paper, putting it even more strongly: "There were just as many organizations in support of equality within the Church," she asserted. "I would strongly challenge that claim," Hawkins countered, noting that anti-racist views were likely held by "a small minority." In summary, he said, the student seemed to be "using evidence to say what she wanted to say," rather than following where it leads.

Hawkins is not mistaken to see a student at times defending her own faith, and Ashley clearly overestimates the prevalence of racial progressivism in the church of that era. Having myself witnessed Ashley's diligent and conscientious work, however—this is the student who returned to her project in August to make corrections—and with more time to peruse her article than Hawkins had in our interview, I feel compelled to point out several places in which she grapples creditably with the pervasiveness of racism. In supporting the idea that white Christians took part in the lynching, she writes, "The sheer number of how many people were witnessed to be in the mob, and the percent of the community that claimed Christian faith, makes a case that white Christians were in the crowd." More important, she acknowledges that the Klan was "a self-proclaimed Protestant organization" and that "the 'white supremacy dogma' was considered 'a God-given right,'" meaning that racism was to some degree intertwined with religious doctrine. She does attempt to draw some separation between these two, pointing to the Christian role in abolitionism and arguing that racism, "which had shaped a society of black inferiority long before even the formation of the KKK, had been deeply embedded into the minds of thousands of people, not just Christians." Ultimately, she judges, it was this widely held belief that "triggered the crowd guilty of the lynching," and it would be unfair to hold the church responsible over and above the racist society of which it was a part. Hawkins prefers to emphasize the degree to which the church is implicated in that racist society, making it more difficult for modern Christians to distance themselves from past actions and calling them to make a more searching self-critique. I agree, but these points take time to grasp, and it seems reasonable for a young Christian, having acknowledged and condemned a culture of "white supremacy" and "black inferiority," to hold these as being in conflict with the religion's core teachings. I see, in the project, a student struggling earnestly to reconcile personal commitments with a troubling history and moving toward more complex historical understandings, albeit with a distance still to go. She and Hawkins share many concerns and commitments, and I believe she would have taken his comments greatly to heart. Sadly, this was a missed opportunity, given that the two never met, but it is helpful in at least envisioning a way in which feedback from outside experts could push students toward more complex historical thinking.

Public value of artifacts

Even when the historians found fault in certain pieces of the students' work, they saw great value in the exhibit as a whole. Considering the tenor of some of Hawkins's remarks, I asked whether there was any *negative* value in making the work available. He replied that "the benefits far outweigh the negatives in terms of being a resource for the community" and that "the only negative" would be if someone "stumbles across the student's interpretation of the church and the lynching, for instance, and takes that as gospel... without understanding that this is a particular interpretation." Asked how troubling he found this prospect, Hawkins said he was "no more concerned" by it than by people's "use of online sources in general." Madison agreed that although he had seen no works of individual brilliance, the overall impact of the work was strikingly positive. Students may not produce interpretations at the level of historians, but, as judged by those historians, even their imperfect work has power.

Three of the four pointed to value in the way the exhibit made information about the lynching more accessible. For Pattengale, this was a crucial respect in which the website added value beyond Madison's book. Comparing the two, he said that the wiki "makes it *much* more accessible." For his part, Madison agreed: "Fifty years ago, no one was telling the story because they were afraid to.... Sixteen- or seventeen-year-old students now tell the story. It's available, it's accessible, it will exist through years, maybe decades, maybe centuries, who knows?" As a public historical virtue, access does have limits. To speak of access is to say nothing about the substance of what has been written or the uses to which it will be put. Nevertheless, Warnock made a strong case for its importance. "I imagine if you were growing up in Marion in the fifties and you asked about the lynching your parents could easily say, you know, 'Nothing happened. Don't talk about it.'" But with this work posted online, the truth would be much harder to suppress: "That's the value of the Internet. You got stuff out there that's available, and you can't cut it off anymore." If students participated in repeated projects, the discussion might go beyond access, toward the sort of questions Alex was most inclined to ask: What does it mean to memorialize? To take accountability? How might we go beyond this, thinking of work as contributing to debates or even framing them? But however it might be enhanced, the value of accessible information, as created in this project, struck the historians as real and meaningful.

Some of the students, as I have noted previously, saw value in the opportunity to formulate and express their own perspectives on the lynching. Professor Madison agreed. While writing his own book, he said, he was acutely aware of his status as an "outsider," for better and for worse. Written by local residents, the students' wiki projects did something he never could: "The beauty... of this project is that it's Marion people who are telling the story. Telling their own story, learning their own story, creating their own story the way they want to tell it." The students may have lacked Madison's critical distance and certainly his deep expertise, but their status as locals gives them a different kind of legitimacy, and their active and creative re-telling of the story makes it a living part of community memory.

The student interviews also showed that the project helped some of them to establish or strengthen relationships in the community. Madison intuited as much from his review of the website, pointing out the value of building relationships with interviewees and changing public perceptions of Marion High School. Looking at Jason's interview, Madison commented on the broader public value of the project:

> Here we have another person [Jason's grandmother] who is not in this class, who is not connected to this school, but who... interacts with the student—who becomes part of the learning process.... I suspect Barbara is going to talk to other people. You know, "I had a student from Marion High School come and interview me and he was really very nice and smart. I had a good experience."

Schools are important institutions in Indiana's small cities and towns, first and foremost through their athletic programs, but Madison saw an opportunity to heighten their status as intellectual centers: "I think getting students out into the community, and getting them out there intellectually engaged, not just as athletes on the basketball court... is value for the community as well as for the student." Beyond making information publicly available, then, and beyond advancing students' individual learning, this work holds the possibility of changing the position of the school in the community. Just as the work helped establish Mr. Munn as a local public intellectual, it could help redefine Marion High School as more fully an institution of public education.

Conclusion

To the extent that the series of interviews reported in this chapter offered an opportunity to evaluate student work by gauging public reaction, the response was encouraging. The projects received a few pointed criticisms, but only one interviewee gave the effort less than positive marks overall. These results are not definitive for several reasons: There are many perspectives that go unrepresented in the interviews; it would be helpful to know more about how and how often the work was actually read online; and the value of the project will always be partially indeterminate, because much depends on the future uses to which the learning is put. Still, the interviews provide ample evidence that students can do work of real value to others

Another goal of the chapter was to demonstrate, test, and refine a process by which such projects can be read, learned from, and thereby brought to fruition—first by identifying the sorts of local figures that might be invited to provide feedback on student work and then by examining how value emerges through their readings and comments. In that respect, the interviews show that numerous resources are available, even in a small community like Marion. Teachers, librarians, clergy, members of the media, public officials, and college professors—all can contribute. Their participation might be difficult to enlist in the course of more traditional history class assignments (not to impugn the generosity of my interviewees, many of whom would gladly help if asked), but the real consequences of public work provide a natural occasion and purpose for conversation. Where existing relationships and networks do not exist, they are waiting to be built: networks of genealogists, history buffs, and other keepers of memory without formal title. Munn and others have done this over many years in Marion. I benefited from their work when arranging interviews and hope that I have, in some small way, helped to advance it. Part of the value of this work comes from the network itself, which continues to bear fruit as people work toward historical understanding and take historically informed civic action. Another aspect of value comes from the fact that schools, teachers, and students would be key participants, embodying a socially engaged form of learning, building connections between classroom and community, and creating ongoing opportunities for civic dialogue.

The greatest shortcoming of the process, as carried out in this chapter, is the lack of any meeting between students and audience members. As I have stated, students would have benefited from seeing the interest that so many readers took in their work and also wrestling with their criticisms. Over and above all of this, it would be helpful for students to experience the sheer variety of ways in which projects can be read and the diverse and sometimes conflicting standards by which work can be judged. School grading scales typically collapse evaluations onto a single axis, with grades assigned by a single reader. When doing consequential work in public, multiple readers must be taken into account, not all can (or should) be made equally happy, and success is not necessarily equal to the sum of their judgments. Learners must keep in mind what they hope to accomplish (even as, in a broader sense, they remain open to new purposes), and they must decide which judgments matter most and which are better sidestepped or disregarded. These are not lessons easily learned, and high school juniors are unlikely to achieve them fully. But as they near adulthood, students would benefit from more learning experiences that call on them to act in complex social situations, weigh a range of evaluations, and clarify their understandings of what really matters.

CONCLUSION

In Marion, in May 2011—while sipping coffee at the Spencer House, if memory serves—I came across a blog entry written by the Harvard scholar and school reformer Richard Elmore, which he had posted to the website EdWeek.org. In his post, Elmore sketches two classes that he says are fairly typical of those encountered in his research. One class is "regular" English; the other, "honors." Much like Sizer before him, Elmore describes the classrooms as uninspiring and intellectually shallow—scenes, alternatingly, of boredom and a kind of contented quiescence.[1] In the "regular" class, a teacher attempts to stimulate discussion, but most students hold side conversations or "[sit] silently, staring into space, waiting for the bell to ring." In "honors" English, students organize their papers, notes, and quizzes into three-ring binders. Elmore comments:

> It is clear that the students are having a good time doing this; it is also clear that they have written a total of about ten pages of prose between January and May; and it is clear that the main reason they are having a good time is that they are forestalling whatever the "work" is for that day. After forty-five minutes of excruciatingly detailed, rule-oriented discussion of what goes where in the portfolio, the teacher suggests that the students spend the next forty minutes silently reading a section of the text. (2011)

According to Elmore, the most demanding classes, like Advanced Placement, move faster, but are fundamentally similar in stressing "volume, coverage, pace, and recall" and in functioning primarily to bring students under "adult control." These problems are longstanding, Elmore acknowledges, and they have been addressed by generations of reformers, but even under a regime of "so called high-stakes accountability," complacency pervades classrooms.

Reading this passage, I was struck not only by the contrast between Elmore's classrooms and those in which I was spending my days, but also by seeing old critiques expressed so forcefully, so far into the age of the Internet and the educational accountability movement. There would surely be many ways to enliven these classrooms, and many teachers succeed with methods different from those I have explored in these pages. And yet, even as a variety of improvements are imaginable, the persistence of these problems is enough to temper expectations for quick, large-scale change. With such cautions in mind, I have attempted to learn from an experiment in one curricular approach—an approach that elevates the creation of value-oriented public products over coverage, recall, and rule-oriented minutia; that attempts to raise the stakes of student work more constructively than an annual test and with greater intellectual substance; and that does so by inducting students into the sort of public discourse to which Elmore contributed with his impassioned post.

Previous chapters have shown how this kind of learning can have valuable educational qualities for both students and their audiences in a way not typically engendered by more traditional history curriculum. In these concluding pages, I reflect on the broader implications of the research and the questions that remain unanswered. How can public learning play out in students' lives over a longer span? What is the likelihood of success when projects address more prosaic topics than the Marion lynching, or when teachers pursue community research under less hospitable circumstances? Where might an interested teacher begin, and what might learning-as-a-service look like outside of local history? Real obstacles stand in the way of more widespread implementation. Bill Munn's style of teaching is noteworthy, in part, because it is so rare and because the dominant system and culture of teaching, learning, and assessment operate under contrary assumptions. At the same time, Deweyan ideas and practices linger in certain parts of the curriculum, and ongoing social and technological trends hold great potential for making student work more public and more valuable. So, while giving due credit to the obstacles, I attempt to articulate a few possible futures for curriculum and teaching, for the development of educational technologies, and for research on public learning.

In my interviews with members of the public, conversation periodically circled back to the projects' possible long-term effects on participating students. Sylvia Williams wondered what sense the students would make of their work several years down the road. As they became adults and parents themselves, would they point to it and tell their children, "This is what I did; this was important to me"? When faced with new injustices, would they recall their projects and think, "I have to speak up about it," or "I can make a difference"? James Madison was generally optimistic about the potential for a lasting impact of this sort, but he also raised the concern that once the students had become mature adults, they might have mixed feelings about seeing their adolescent work on permanent display. Because I have not sought out Munn's former students to inquire about the work's long-term effects, such questions lie mostly outside the purview of the book. Still, this seems an appropriate place to step back and consider the broader implications of the pedagogical approach. As it happened, I did cross paths with one CHP alumnus who had a story to tell. One Saturday at the end of the project, while meeting students at the public library for final interviews, I happened to meet an old high school classmate, Ramon Volz. We had not spoken in many years, but when I explained why I was in town, he launched eagerly into stories of his own CHP oral history, vividly recollected even thirteen years after the fact. I proceeded to question him much as I did the current year's students, and his memories touched on nearly every theme identified in earlier chapters of this book, providing a kind of corroboration and placing one project in the context of a longer life trajectory.

When first given the assignment in 1998 to interview someone about life during World War II, Ramon said he hadn't known where to begin. Mr. Munn suggested he talk with Elton Vice, a former POW whose story Munn wanted to record. Ramon explained the difficulty: "It was out of my comfort zone. 'Cause I was really shy, [to] talk to a stranger, talk to somebody way older than me that had been in a war, talk to him about something I had no idea about, other than what we learned in books." There was little reason to worry. Vice went on for ninety minutes, filling both sides of the cassette. Ramon was able to recall the interview in detail: Vice speaking about his life before the war, his service in France, the barn where he hid from Nazis, his capture, and his eventual return.[2] Especially memorable was one artifact that Vice had brought home from battle—a German flag. Said Ramon, "They would kill a Nazi soldier. Somebody would check it for a bomb... and then they would search the body for anything else that would be on it, anything they could use. And they found a Nazi flag on one guy, so they took it, and they all signed it." Remarkably, Vice donated the flag to the CHP along with his medals, patches, and pencil sketches of the cities he had visited. Ramon recalled talking with Munn about how the flag would be best displayed—in a Plexiglas case, they decided, to show the signatures on both sides—and later seeing it on display at the entrance of the library's local history museum. Public contribution and recognition were both important to Ramon, as they were to most of the students I worked with. His project was one of eleven featured in the CHP book, *Rough Times* (Munn, Bratton, & Lakes, 1999), but another sort of publication, Munn's newspaper column, elicited a stronger reaction. "I got a call one day that Mr. Munn had cited me in one of his works.... I was like, '*That's amazing*.'" He looked back on his interview with obvious pride, calling it "the best project I've ever done," even compared with those from college, none of which "ever hit that close to home."

A full accounting of Ramon's learning would echo points from previous chapters. To name just a few: He described the interview as powerfully "intimate" and marveled at the difference between textbook knowledge of World War II and a firsthand interview. He also remembered learning how to "back up [the interviewee's] story with sources" and to place their experiences in historical context. Ramon volunteered all of this and more with little prodding on my part, but I pressed on one more speculative point. In the 1990s, Mr. Munn had supervised an elective class explicitly designated as "service-learning," which Ramon took during his senior year, assisting a local elementary school teacher and hoping for another "magical" experience. That semester's service lacked the intense emotional impact of his oral history, but its consequences were far reaching. Ramon went on to Indiana State University, where, based partly on that experience, he studied elementary education. At the time of our 2011 meeting, Ramon was teaching a second-grade Spanish class in a dual-immersion school in Fort Wayne. When teaching social studies, he said, he still encouraged students to talk with family members about their life experiences, a practice he explicitly linked to his CHP interview. Ramon's project clearly figured constructively in his life course, helping him to summon personal self-confidence and to develop a sense of what work he found meaningful, and then leading into subsequent educational experiences that have become his life's work.

Curricular possibilities

The particular circumstances of the Marion lynching permeate the students' work and my discussion of it here. As a result, every conclusion is circumscribed by the question of whether other projects on other topics would yield similar results. Madison raised this issue in my interview with him, noting the unique power of the lynching photograph in generating interest. Taking an earlier student project on Marion's Memorial Coliseum as an example of a more commonplace topic, Madison weighed the relative pedagogical possibilities. Such a project would not be "nearly as emotional," but he saw potential for it to yield significant moments of insight: "There is something in my community, and I've driven by that all my life—but wait a minute, it has some meaning. And a generation long before mine built that, and has used it and named it Memorial. Memorial to what?" Even a project on such a building, he estimated, offers a greater chance of "long-term consequences" when compared with the traditional term paper.[3] In every interview in which the issue arose, including those with Margaret Davis, Tim Eckerle, and Becky Boyle, public interviewees agreed that projects on other topics would be worthwhile. As to Madison's specific comparison, my impression, based on other projects I have read or witnessed, is that locally significant buildings—factories, public facilities, and some noteworthy residences like the designs of Samuel Plato—do hold this kind of interest, at least when personal connections can be made. Owing to that personal dimension, oral histories are probably more consistently meaningful than reports on buildings.[4] At the outset of this book, I stipulated that the Marion lynching is a topic of unusual importance and an extreme case relative to most other instances of student research. This is undoubtedly true in terms of its historical significance and the depth of reflections it calls forth from students and audience members. Still, it would be a mistake to assume that other projects would not be viable from the perspective of viewer interest. Many people are reluctant to engage emotionally with a topic as distressing as the lynching and, on a day-to-day basis, would rather learn about topics that evoke pride rather than shame. Here, again, there are tensions between nostalgia, boosterism, and critical history. These tensions will never be fully resolved but might best be negotiated by a teacher with an eye for intriguing topics that give voice to marginal perspectives on local historical experience, setting the context for harder hitting commentary.

Even granting that a topic like Memorial Coliseum presents a profitable opportunity for student work, one might wonder whether such locally significant subjects would eventually run dry, especially if projects were undertaken by more than a few classes per school. A look through the CHP archives does show that as schools, hospitals, and post offices were treated and the number of outstanding public buildings dwindled, the share of reports on students' own houses rose. Many such buildings hold little significance, and the reports read as litanies of buyers, sellers, and architectural features that demonstrate little in the way of interpretative complexity. More typically, though, one story leads to another, and research begets more research. This is the answer that Munn gave when I raised the question, and I have seen it confirmed throughout my involvement. As a teacher listens to interviews and reads papers, he or she can develop a fuller knowledge and more nuanced understanding of the local past, learning about significant events, people, places, stories, and questions that would make for good projects. As the teacher and the class build a reputation and a local network, people approach with stories—as when family members suggested topics to me or when Munn solicited new leads and sources through his newspaper columns. Each crop of new students brings with them new friends and relations who can illuminate different corners of history. Human historical experience is essentially an inexhaustible resource. Each vertical file, each microfilm reel, each shoebox of photographs holds forgotten stories, and even if only a fraction prove to be of broad interest, this provides ample opportunity for research.

Ramon's interview with Elton Vice shows Munn drawing from a kind of personal research agenda, and during my time in Marion, I also kept a lengthy list of research ideas. To imagine such an agenda as something akin to a checklist, though, fails to capture the proliferation of meanings that makes topics so plentiful. The details of daily life often appear mundane, to students or to interviewees, but set against other interviews and secondary sources from fields like social and cultural history, a teacher—or the students, or the interviewees themselves—can recognize new significances. New projects can also relate to old ones in a variety of ways, with each new cohort of students extending, qualifying, reinterpreting, or taking issue with what has come before. One investigation of Mary Ball does not "use up" the topic but establishes a field against which further research can be set, as witnessed in the successive projects of James Madison, Cynthia Carr, and the student I have called Emily. They can be addressed to new audiences or written for new occasions—say, an anniversary, a play opening, or an election—all of which calls for creative re-framing.

Pedagogical possibilities

In the current educational environment, I do not expect that a community history project could easily be implemented in every classroom, but it could be implemented successfully by some, to some degree, and this process could generate ideas, conversations, and supporting tools to make it more feasible for others. How might an interested teacher begin? Based on what I have seen in Marion, an interview project offers the best chances for initial success. A teacher might specify one or two themes—veterans of a certain war, the history of the school, or experiences of segregation and the civil rights movement. Students would identify potential interviewees, hold preliminary conversations with them to scope out topics, draft and revise sets of open-ended questions, collect consent forms, and record interviews. The projects would then be published in some form—online, ideally, on one of the many free video-sharing websites available, though, as a first step, they could also be shown to parents or classmates. Students would write short papers or deliver presentations introducing and contextualizing specific interview clips. Many guides and resources are available for this type of instruction.[5] The crucial point, from the perspective of this book, would be for the teacher to push toward more public audiences and to continually guide students back to the question of how they can best make a contribution.

An oral history project is manageable, maximizes the likelihood of high-impact personal encounters, and engages students in academic writing and analysis while creating real value for families, communities, and the public. If teachers have some students capable of working more independently, they could begin by taking inventory of local history topics and sources. They might, like one of Munn's early classes, scan through old microfilm or vertical files or ask town elders about important events, then assess the various topics' significance, research feasibility, and public appeal. They could look to historical websites, museums, and other works of public history for inspiration. Future classes could then begin working from the leads they had generated. Other community members could be enlisted as needs arose or as they saw opportunities to contribute and learn.

Projects of this sort benefit a great deal from the skills and knowledge that a teacher can build over time, but it is possible to start down the pathway with relatively little expertise. To undertake an oral history project, a teacher should have familiarity with mobile audio and video recording apps, a basic understanding of the purposes of oral history, and, most important, an attitude of flexibility when dealing with inevitable snags. More advanced capacities can be developed through successive iterations of a project. Reflecting on the first few experiences, a teacher might develop a better sense of how to guide question writing, improve recording quality, and edit video files for public display. Like Munn, they might also begin to fill in their personal understandings of which historical experiences are significant in the lives of students, their families, and their communities. For Munn, in small-town Indiana this has meant asking questions such as: Who are students related to and what have those relatives experienced? What meaningful physical landmarks do students pass frequently and unthinkingly? What religious communities and other outside groups do they belong to? What historical narratives are most significant to those communities, and which would be meaningful for students to participate in re-telling? A motivated teacher might also feel the need to place these events in context to show their relevance to broader historical issues. Even for regional topics, literature in social and cultural history presents many possibilities for building bridges between secondary school classrooms and scholarly communities. To the extent that it is unrealistic to expect teachers to quickly become familiar with relevant, accessible secondary literature, then librarians, college history students, or teachers in training might welcome the opportunity to curate resource guides—perhaps as a part of their own course projects or professional responsibilities.

Besides helping with the completion of local history projects, I suspect that this sort of learning would have positive spillover effects on other aspects of teaching practice—if not inevitably, then with the aid of guided reflection and discussion. It stands to reason that teachers' understanding of the value of history would factor in their ability to stimulate student interest. By undertaking repeated projects, observing audience responses, and discussing what makes them more or less successful, a teacher might learn to cultivate meaningful, generative, and intellectually engaging project assignments and to connect features of student work—use of evidence, quality of writing, topic selection, and so on—to the project's goals and its ultimate success. More generally, teachers might become more sensitive to the various facets of their subject's power and appeal: the tactile immediacy of a document, the pleasures of narrative, the moral force of historical evidence, and the ability of history to inform contemporary debates.

Research and development

Community history research has become much easier over time, in large part because of technological developments. In the 1990s, recording oral history projects presented numerous logistical challenges. Cassette recorders often broke, tapes became tangled, and analog recordings were difficult to store, copy, and edit. Most interviews from the early years of the CHP still sit in boxes, and even into the first generation of digital recording, files are in-consistent formats, scattered across hard drives and outdated storage media like floppy disks and Zip drives. Creating a printed book in the 1990s was an almost prohibitively difficult task. Having attempted it once, Munn let it be known that he would never do so again.

During the ensuing two decades, the situation changed dramatically. Today, most students carry in their pockets recording devices (if not tripods or external microphones) that surpass the quality of those available in the 1990s. Digital files are quickly transferred and easily backed up to cloud storage. Online databases and secondary sources have become more accessible, and digital publication tools—blogs, wikis, video-sharing services, content management systems—make it ever easier to get one's products in front of an audience. These trends are likely to continue, and public learning seems to be well served by the general thrust of technological change, which supports the creation and sharing of digital media. To date, CHP work has focused on text articles and recorded interviews, but it has occasionally reached into print publication, documentary video, image galleries, maps, time lines, physical exhibits, and interactive media. All are ripe for further experimentation. Video editing is becoming considerably more accessible, making it easier to pull together thematically related clips from multiple interviews into short documentaries. Mobile applications represent another promising frontier. With the right software, local residents could be allowed to read articles about nearby locations on smartphones, or students could design walking or driving tours of historic sites.[6]

As new publishing formats become popular, there will be new opportunities to re-interpret and re-present historical content. Always in search of new outlets, Munn has taken a longstanding interest in blogging and podcasting, and in retirement he has nurtured an active Facebook group, "Disappearing Marion," around issues of local historic preservation. Tools like this, which allow for subscription and group membership, would help a class cultivate subscribers and channels for publicizing new work—a growing necessity in towns like Marion as local newspaper coverage declines. They would also provide opportunities for students to see what kind of history captures public attention, with immediate feedback coming through viewership statistics and comments left by readers. Feedback mechanisms of this sort might be designed to strengthen students' connection to their audiences, help them gauge and weigh feedback, and reinforce their sense of their own contributions.

Feedback tools could form one subject of a program of research and development that would work toward understanding and facilitating value development, both in the developmental trajectories of individual students and as shared cultural processes operating over longer time spans. A program of value-oriented curriculum research might attempt to identify what sorts of values can be created through activity in various disciplines—not with the intention of developing a fixed list or constraining teachers' and students' exercise of judgment and creativity, but to support projects most likely to provide satisfying, educative experiences. I have begun to do so here, in history. Researchers might then, by documenting and writing about those values across a variety of cases, begin to build shared, nuanced understandings of the shades that various valuations can take, the ways in which they are learned, and the enduring questions that surround them. At the same time, the curriculum researcher and designer might seek to identify ways in which these values can be appreciated by learners, basically but authentically, and then to refine practices in which learners can participate, increasing over time their abilities to contribute publicly even as they develop a stake in the communities they are serving, and, through reflection and review, deepening their understandings in the multifaceted ways that I have described.

Researchers might assess the existing curriculum, seeking instances in which the specified subject matter is best addressed in the course of value-producing activities. The Common Core State Standards, for example, place great stock in teaching students to modulate their writing to fit purposes and audiences. The standards for literacy in history/social studies (and other subjects outside the traditional language arts) specify that students should be able to "adapt their communication in relation to audience, task, purpose and discipline." They should also "appreciate nuances, such as how the composition of an audience should affect tone when speaking." Most important, they should come to "value evidence," recognizing the importance of "documentary evidence in history" (Common Core State Standards Initiative, 2010, p. 7).[7] These objectives are well addressed by the sort of project described in these pages, and I submit that they would be difficult to teach, learn, or assess as effectively using more traditional means. Researchers might also take stock of the values being created by the curriculum as a whole, look for what is missing, and then seek to redress the gaps. They might, for example, look at what was not achieved by the lynching project: a sense of continuity between past and present injustices, links between argument and value, and in some cases critical reading and writing skills.

They might, then, create and refine tools or practices—such as questions to guide reflection and review—that would help to improve work products and be taken up by students and teachers with increasingly nuanced understanding over time. Review and evaluation were at the heart of the interviews reported in Chapter 5, but they played only a peripheral role in student work during the project. (One student created a guide to resources on the lynching, for example, making judgments about which were most useful. Reading that project, one librarian noted that the student had done a service by summarizing and reviewing the material.) This strikes me as especially fertile ground for experimentation. By asking students to review each other's projects and those of their predecessors (possibly in private, to protect sensitivities), a teacher could facilitate conversations about the standards by which historical work should be judged, helping students to refine capacities for critical judgment and to imagine responses to their own work. Assuming that some projects will always be more successful than others, this sort of review could help to train public attention on interesting, high-quality work. Review also suggests ways of applying a pedagogy of public value beyond local history. Students might publish online reviews of historical books, articles, films, or documentaries, which could, in turn, direct other students to learning materials. Unlike some of the more in-depth projects proposed above, review could be done in small increments, as a way of incorporating public work throughout the school year, posing questions of value in relation to topics across the curriculum, and priming students to undertake projects of their own. The process of writing reviews would foreground the sense in which students' historical interpretations are public productions—actions taken in and through a shared culture with consequences for others who inhabit it.

One of the most striking aspects of Lawrence Beitler's photograph of the Marion lynching is the way it demonstrates, on several levels at once, how viewers of an event participate in constructing its meaning (Figure 1, introduction). Part of the grotesquery of any lynching derives from the suffering inflicted upon its victims, but the larger significance of the practice is bound up in its status as a public spectacle and in the message of white supremacy that it projects. Because of this, the meaning of lynching lies in and substantially depends upon spectators' interpretations and responses. The Beitler photograph shows, starkly, the complicity of some who were physically present that night in August 1930. The various crowd members' gestures and facial expressions, whether menacing or chillingly nonchalant, are essential to the meaning of the image, and one man, who stares into the camera and points toward the bodies above his head, is at least a secondary subject. His significance is attested to by a copy of the photograph that is reprinted in *Without Sanctuary*, accompanied by a lock of hair and the handwritten caption "Bo pointn to his niga" (Allen, 2000, p. 84).

The photograph documents the complicity of these spectators, then, but it does more than that: The photographer is himself an important participant, and viewers of the photograph become implicated as well. Photography was a common element of the lynching ritual, serving to create a persistent representation of the event that could be circulated, through postcards and newspaper printings, to far more people than had witnessed the original act—people whose collaboration would be necessary if the social order were to be perpetuated. By composing the image in a particular way, the photographer could also contribute to its meaning. Anthony W. Lee notes that photographs often include a figure who serves as a "surrogate" for viewers, instructing them in "a proper regard for the scene" (quoted in Apel & Smith, 2007, p. 6). In Beitler's photograph, the pointing man is most clearly demonstrative. (Modern viewers can hardly help but have their attention directed by his outstretched hand, but assuming that most would recoil at the thought of directly identifying with him, this shows that multiple interpretations remain possible.) Viewers have reacted in many different ways, with some redistributing the image, writing captions, or purchasing copies that would be secreted away and passed on to later generations. Surely some viewers gave their tacit or explicit approval whereas some quietly disagreed and still others were moved to resistance, like the editors of the *Chicago Defender* and possibly the writer of "Strange Fruit," Abel Meeropol.

Twenty-first-century viewers, adults or children, are by no means exempt from responsibility. When examining the photograph and learning about its historical context, they, too, must interpret and react in one way or another. Those reactions have consequences—whether a viewer quickly looks away, putting the event out of mind, or whether he or she instead reflects on its implications for present-day social conditions and then shares those insights with others. The same could be said of learning about other topics in history, though, to be sure, not all will command so intense a response. This is the broadest implication of this book: By conceiving of learning as creative action taken within a shared, public culture, and by judging that work on the basis of its value to that culture, we would better convey the importance of learning and would encourage adults and children to take fuller responsibility for its social and ethical consequences.

Arguing about values

Some of the values I have identified in this book are relatively incontrovertible. Regarding others, or their relative importance, people will inevitably disagree, as Tom, David, Ashley, and Alex would disagree over issues of fact, emotion, and bias, or as others would disagree about the proper way to memorialize an atrocity. Our local work in the classroom and community that spring had a mixed record at provoking this kind of argument. It can claim one unplanned debate early on—heated but not especially edifying—and some argumentative papers. With other students the project failed, in some sense, to demonstrate the value of argument. The best example of constructive argument in Mr. Munn's room that spring came not from the classes in which I participated, but from his single section of twelfth-grade government, sandwiched between two of eleventh-grade history. Several times, I returned in the afternoon to find Munn invigorated by debates in that class. He was making use of the PBS series *Justice*, which is based on the philosopher Michael Sandel's renowned Harvard undergraduate class and which carries the tagline, "What's the right thing to do?" (2011). Munn would play the video as Sandel set out thought experiments and moral dilemmas, then pause it to facilitate class discussion on the ethical responses and, ultimately, the meaning of justice.

Sandel's brilliantly Socratic series is, among other things, further justification for a pluralistic approach to pedagogy (and to ethics, besides), but I remain hopeful that future research can clarify and strengthen the role of argument in value-oriented work and offer more guidance for how teachers might address it in a project like the CHP. This book began with a quotation from the novelist and historian Wallace Stegner. In his final novel, taking the voice of an aged professor of literature, Stegner wistfully recalls, "Our hottest arguments were always about how we could *contribute*" (1987, p. 11, emphasis in original). In the curricular approach I have discussed, it seems to me, the underlying question requires only a slight modification of the one Sandel poses: "What's the valuable thing to contribute?" or, more succinctly, "What should we value?"

Coffeehouses, public squares, publications, libraries, and public schools are all important components of our public sphere, where private citizens can come together and deliberate on issues of shared concern. They are also historical contingencies. Most of these public spaces arose in eighteenth-century Europe, and the public school even more recently (Habermas, 1989). Their future is uncertain, and they must continually be remade. I find it difficult to drive down Marion's main road, the bypass, without sensing a public decline in which the square is superseded by spaces like the mall and then the Walmart—corporate spaces that also, in their uniformity, deny any organic historicity and sense of place. There is cause for hope, as well—in certain participatory features of the networked society or in the recent revitalization of city centers after decades of sterile suburbanization. In Marion, however, few of these trends have taken hold. In a 2011 dispatch from the town, broadcast on NPR's *Morning Edition*, Marion's mayor discussed a plan to close as many as seventeen neighborhood parks while working to attract major chains like "Target, Texas Roadhouse [and] Panera" (Adams, 2011).

The communitarian sensibility that informs the CHP can be tinged with nostalgia. It shows, at times, a tendency to glorify the past uncritically, filtering memories through the lens of a whitewashed, Disneyesque Main Street, USA (Frantz & Collins, 2000). I am not entirely immune to this myself. But the subject matter of this book warns against such backward-looking romanticization. The bodies, the tree, the photograph all serve as reminders of a concerted campaign of exclusion from public life. That campaign led people like Sylvia Williams—even as she walked to a school that an earlier generation had named for Horace Mann—to bend her path out and around the square. Ultimately, this book raises a challenge: to move forward in the light of this history, humbled, informed, emboldened, and compelled, and to build new ways of learning that create and reflect public values, while nurturing new citizens to carry them forward.

APPENDIX: RESEARCH DESIGN

This appendix provides details of research design and data collection, focusing on the interviews with students and community members that are reported in Chapters 4 and 5, respectively. After explaining how each set of interviews was conducted, I discuss the strengths and limitations of the evidence and the kind of claims it does and does not permit. Interview protocols are included at the end of the appendix.

Student interviews

Each student took part in two audiotaped interviews: one at the beginning of the project and another after it was complete. The initial interviews were conducted during my first two weeks at Marion High School and served several purposes: to begin building rapport with the students, to gather background information about them and their interests, to establish how long they and their families had lived in Marion, and to probe their background knowledge about the lynching. Students were interviewed individually in an empty room down the hall from Bill Munn's classroom. I attempted to interview students before they began new learning about the lynching, but this was not always possible. All had heard some basic information about the lynching when they volunteered to participate in the project, several had begun to thumb through copies of James Madison's *A Lynching in the Heartland* (2001), and one had attended the lynching play *The Gospel According to James* before being interviewed. As a result, although the interviews indicate that students lacked detailed knowledge of the lynching events, they do not allow for a formal pre-test/post-test analysis and were not formally coded. They are cited only occasionally in the text, typically to supply context about students' interests and backgrounds or to establish the degree of continuity or change in their attitudes or abilities over the course of the project.

The bulk of the evidence cited in Chapter 4 comes from the second set of formal student interviews, which were conducted during the final week of the school year and the first week of the summer, after each student had completed his or her project. Some interviews took place during school hours in the same empty room in which the initial interviews were conducted. One was conducted in the school library, and all others took place in a private study room at the public library. To ensure full participation as summer break began, students who attended interviews outside school hours were offered fifteen-dollar gift cards.

The final interviews were designed to elicit students' understandings of the project with a particular eye toward the perceived value of their work, its public nature, and students' reflections on race and the history of their community. The interviews began with each student being shown a copy of his or her wiki project and asked to give a brief "tour" of the project. Students were then asked to elaborate by explaining which part of the work they would most want someone to see, how people had reacted when viewing their wiki page, and which moments during the project were most memorable and most frustrating. Next, the interviews moved into a comparative section. In Bill Munn's class first semester, the students had written papers that were of similar scope to the year-end wiki projects but were not focused on the local community or written for a public audience. In this more traditional academic paper, students selected, researched, and wrote about a topic in U.S. history prior to the Civil War. I printed these papers and presented them to the students during the interview. They were offered time to re-familiarize themselves with their papers and were then asked to describe the experience of working on that earlier paper and to compare the two projects. I began with general questions, and then if students did not comment on specific issues, the questions became increasingly directive. For example, students were first asked, "What, if anything, is valuable about each project?" By the end of this section, if students had not commented on the public nature of the project, I asked, "What was good and bad about having your work end up on WikiMarion instead of just being handed in to the teacher for a grade?" I pressed for both good and bad features of the project, and if students emphasized positive features in their initial response, as most did, I asked again for downsides. The late stages of each interview asked for students' views on race, history, and their hometown—questions that elicited some of their deepest reflections. I concluded each interview by asking students what advice they would offer to others starting a similar project. Interview transcripts were analyzed using a process of open coding, after which related codes were combined or grouped under superordinate codes and used to identify significant themes. This coding process was informed by the concerns running throughout the book with special attention given to statements about the different sorts and degrees of value found in the project. Nevertheless, I attempted to be responsive to unexpected or emergent themes, such as student comments about the added stress that attended public work or its effects on their college applications.

This interview method has a number of potential limitations with respect to the kinds of claims that it does and does not allow. First, students' responses were produced in the context of the interview and must be interpreted as such. They do not necessarily reflect preexisting understandings, reached during their work on the project itself, and some of the understandings they expressed would not have been achieved—or expressed in the same way—without this opportunity for structured reflection. Nevertheless, students' responses do indicate the types of understandings that might be achieved through this sort of work. The end of the project was fairly rushed and did not include any formal reflection; one implication is that the process should make room for students to pause and look back on what they have accomplished and then ahead to worthy next projects.

A more significant issue involves the status differential between the students and me as an interviewer. I played no role in grading the students or their work, and students called me by my first name. In the interview, I emphasized that there were no "right answers" and that I simply wanted to understand their experiences. Still, I was an adult, a former teacher (in another region of the country), and a Stanford doctoral student. I had worked with the students on their projects, and during the project Munn and I necessarily spoke in ways that conveyed the premise that students could do valuable public work. I was likely seen as an authority figure, to some degree, and students may have given what they thought were desired responses or responses that showed their projects in a positive light. I was often surprised by the depth of students' responses and their apparent sincerity, and I wondered whether they would speak to their teenage friends about the project so earnestly (and if not, which of their statements would be more "true").

Despite these limitations, there are several reasons students' explicit statements might be counted as evidence of learning: In some cases, they made especially detailed or insightful comments that stand, in and of themselves, as evidence of the knowledge gained or understandings achieved. That is to say, these students did not simply agree with a statement that was put to them; they explained their project's value vividly and at length, or they elaborated in ways that were specifically related to the details of their own work. Some quotations show moments of profound realization that, although they capture only a single point in time, have a depth that suggests enduring intellectual change of a sort difficult to ascertain from standardized measures or value-added scores. This is the case when Hannah reflects on the place of race in the history of the community and her religious denomination. Briefer statements or less detailed explanations provide weaker evidence, but these can still be noteworthy if a cluster of students is seen to have made similar comments. In some cases, such as the academic performance of the student referred to as David, a single episode seems to owe a great deal to skills or proclivities that a student brought to the project rather than something learned afresh. Even in these cases, the project provided an opportunity to apply skills or ideas in new ways, extend them to new situations, or think about them with greater nuance, but the learning is of a different and less dramatic kind.

It is worth repeating that I do not claim to provide simple, conclusive proof that our efforts in the spring of 2011 succeeded. Some student projects yielded better products or deeper insights than did others, and because assessments of value are ultimately contestable, readers are sure to reach different conclusions about their relative merits. For all of the reasons identified in the book's introduction, I am not an impartial observer, but taken as a whole I believe that the totality of evidence presented in Chapter 4 reflects well on the project, showing a degree of personal engagement with history that would be rare in more traditional assignments. More to the point of my broader argument, the projects and student reflections provide a sense of the risks associated with such work and the variety of ways in which it can create value for students and others.

Community member interviews

The evidence presented in Chapter 5 is drawn primarily from semistructured interviews with observers from outside Marion High School. As above, the primary purpose of these interviews was to elicit evaluations of the work from a range of potential audience members, a list of whom is provided in Chapter 5. I began these sessions by explaining the project and website and letting interviewees orient themselves in the lynching wiki page, at first encouraging them to click on links that interested them. Because subjects began reading from the top of the exhibit's main webpage, articles linked from higher on the page were initially clicked most frequently. To counteract this tendency and to ensure that all student pages received multiple readers, I guided interviewees to specific pages as the interview unfolded. I also directed them to projects close to their areas of expertise—for instance, pointing a local prosecutor to the page on legal depositions, because I knew him to have read the depositions himself. Finally, I attempted to show each interviewee a range of work that varied in terms of both quality and project type. If one of them had seen two oral-history style projects, I next directed him or her to a page based on original sources; if someone had seen a project I considered especially well written, I pointed to a page that struck me as falling short in that area.

I asked interviewees to speak freely, voicing their reactions to what they saw, and to read aloud periodically so that I would know what passages they were examining. After giving an interviewee time to develop a sense of each individual project, I asked for a general evaluation of the work. After an interviewee had examined a number of projects in detail—usually four or five, as time permitted—and scrolled briefly through a few others, I asked for a general sense of the exhibit's quality and of what value it had, if any. Finally, as before, I showed the community members copies of the students' first-semester term papers and asked them to compare the value of the two sorts of projects. The question functioned slightly differently across the two types of interviews. The students had direct knowledge of the first-semester papers—having actually written them—and they tended to make more concrete comparisons. None of the community members more than glanced over the first-semester papers, so their comparisons were based on a more abstracted notion of what a term paper is. Here it is especially clear that the question served as a device for spurring thought and analysis, and that its use does not constitute a comparative research design.

Marion is a small world, and many of these interviewees are connected to one another and to Mr. Munn or the CHP. In particular, many of them have been involved in historical work in the community, and three have had children in Mr. Munn's classes (James Luttrul, Tim Eckerle, and Sylvia Williams). This informs their understanding of the project, but it also means that few were fully impartial. More than the general population, these interviewees also tended to be well informed about local history and the lynching. A few "average citizens" were approached, but it was difficult to find ones willing to be interviewed. I suspect this was because they found the event distasteful or because, despite the option of anonymity, they were reluctant to comment on a sensitive topic about which they had no particular expertise. This amounts to a limitation of both the project and my research. Participants in Marion's local history community consider the event important, and as historical events go, the lynching has generated sustained interest, locally, regionally, and nationally. My interviewees were extremely well positioned to evaluate the project's value; if a historian like Madison, an editor like Breen, and a librarian like Davis can point to specific contributions, this is strong positive evidence. The interviews also show *how* these interviewees evaluated the work—on what grounds and to what standards. Yet there are many perspectives that go unrepresented, and many local citizens may prefer not to learn about it, or at least not to discuss it publicly. Thus, the interviews do not provide a good indication of popular interest in the work or the future uses to which it will be put. The assessment of value here depends, more than usual, on the significance of the work and the importance that it cannot be "swept under the rug," as Rev. Dr. Warnock put it. Over the course of a longer-term project like the CHP, one would hope to see other projects garner more widespread attention.

Protocol for Initial Student Interview

Introduction: The goal of this interview is to help me get to know you better. I want to know a little about you and to understand how you feel about history, history classes, and Marion. I'd also like to know what you've heard about the lynching that took place in Marion.

- This interview doesn't have any right or wrong answers.
- I'll be making a recording of this interview for research purposes. You'll be given a fictitious name if I quote from it in a report or publication.

- Have you read and signed the assent form? And has your parent signed the permission form?
- The interview will take about thirty minutes.
- You don't have to answer any questions that make you uncomfortable, and you can end the interview at any time.

Please say your name for the recording.

1. First, I want to get to know you better. Would you take me through what you did in a typical recent weekend day? [Provide an example if necessary.]
2. How long have you lived in Marion?
3. Where does your family come from? How long has your family lived in Marion?
4. What words come to mind when you think about Marion? Why? Tell me more about that.
5. Are there any other important things about you that you haven't already mentioned? Any clubs or hobbies? Do you make time for friends?
6. Here are some cards with the names of school subjects. Would you arrange them in order of how much you like them? Why do you have—first? Why did you put history where you did?
7. There was once a lynching that took place in Marion. Have you ever heard people talk about a lynching? What did you hear them say?
8. Some people have heard a lot about this lynching. Other people haven't heard very much. Would you tell me the story of that event, as you think it happened?
9. Where else have you learned about the lynching?
10. How are attitudes toward race in Marion? Why do you think that is?
11. Are there places or situations where people definitely would not talk about the lynching? Where?
12. Are there any other big events in Marion's history that you've heard of? What?

Final Student Interview Protocol

Introduction: The goal of this interview is to help me understand how you feel about the project, what you've learned from the project, and how you think about history, history classes, Marion, and its history.

- This interview doesn't have any right or wrong answers.
- I'll be making a recording of this interview for research purposes. You'll be given a fictitious name if I quote from it in a report or publication.
- Have you read and signed the assent form? And has your parent signed the permission form?
- You don't have to answer any questions that make you uncomfortable, and you can end the interview at any time.

So, you've finished the whole project now. Let's look at your project. [Pull up article on WikiMarion, on computer screen.]

1. Give me a quick tour. If someone came to your project online, what would you most want them to see? What are you most proud of? What did you leave out?
2. Tell me about a memorable moment or incident in the project.
3. Tell me about a frustrating or disappointing moment in the project.
4. Have you shown this project to anyone? How did they react? What were they interested in?
5. Here's a copy of the paper you wrote in this class first semester. What did you actually do for that project? What was the best thing? The hardest? How would you compare that project with this one? What, if anything, was valuable about each project? Was one project more valuable than the other?
6. What was good and bad about working on this project? [Use prompts below if a student doesn't comment on a particular aspect.]
   a. How is this project valuable to you personally?
   b. What did you learn while doing this project? What else?
   c. What was good and bad about having your work end up on WikiMarion instead of just being handed in to the teacher for a grade?
7. What adjectives/words would you use to describe history? Why?
8. After completing this project, how do you feel about Marion? What words come to mind when you think about Marion? How is that different from the way you felt before this project?
9. How are attitudes toward race in Marion? Why do you think that is? (Or, why do you think things are the way they are?)
10. What advice would you give to a student starting a project like this?

Community Member Interview Protocol

Introduction: For about fifteen years, students in a U.S. history class at Marion High School have done research on local history and published their results online or at the Marion Public Library. They've done projects on a variety of topics, such as oral histories of the Great Depression, a Veterans' History Project, and significant buildings in Grant County. Last year, a group of students created an online exhibit about a lynching that took place in Marion in 1930. The main goal of this interview is to help me understand your reaction to the students' project. And I'm talking to you because—.

I'll start by asking some questions about you and what you've heard in the past about the lynching. Then we'll move on to the students' projects. Okay, before we begin, here are a few things to remember:

- This interview doesn't have any right or wrong answers.
- I'll be making a recording of this interview for research purposes. If I quote from it in a report or publication, would you prefer to be given a pseudonym or referred to using your real name?
- This interview will take about forty-five to sixty minutes.
- You don't have to answer any questions that make you uncomfortable, and you can end the interview at any time.
- Have you read and signed the consent form?

1. As I explained, I'm gathering reactions to this project from a variety of people in the community, and I'd like to understand how you fit into the community—where you work, what organizations you're involved with, and that kind of thing. So, can you take me through a typical week? What are some of the major things you do in a week?

Probes: What organizations, if any, do you belong to in the community? What activities do you participate in? Do you make time to be with friends?

2. How long have you lived in Marion? How far back does your family go around this area? Do you have any family in town?
3. Okay, as I've mentioned there was once a lynching that took place in Marion. I'd like to understand what you may already know about the event. Have you ever heard people talk about a lynching? What have you heard?

4. Now, we'll look at a project created by students in a class at Marion High School. I'll let you look at the project, and as you look, tell me out loud what you're thinking.

[If necessary, remind subject to keep talking aloud. After about five minutes spent on a single page in the exhibit, prompt the person to look at a different page. Present a spectrum of student work.]

5. Now that you've had a chance to look at some different parts of the project, tell me what you think of it. What have you learned from the project? As a student project, what's good about it? What's bad? What kind of value does this have for the community?
6. [Hand them a history paper.] Here's a term paper that a student wrote in the same class first semester. What is valuable about that kind of project? What is worthwhile? What are the strengths and weaknesses? How would you compare these two projects?
7. [Ask the following if the interviewee dislikes particular aspects of the article covering the lynching.] The rest of this website contains articles on other topics about Marion's history, such as life during the Great Depression. Leaving aside the exhibit on the lynching, how valuable is the rest of the website?
8. What's your overall impression of this project?
9. Is there anything else you'd like to mention?

NOTES

Introduction

1. The photograph has been used consistently through the century, including in recent years. In 1992, it appeared, controversially, on the cover of a single by the rap group Public Enemy—a sardonic comment on the Indiana rape conviction of boxer Mike Tyson (Madison, 2001, pp. 113–116). It was shown in the civil rights documentary *Eyes on the Prize* (Vecchione, 1986) and in a later PBS documentary on photographic history, *American Photography: A Century of Images* (Hovde & Meyer, 1999). It appears twice on facing pages of the collection *Without Sanctuary*, once alongside a lock of hair and misattributed to the city of Joplin, Missouri (Allen, 2000). A magnified and closely cropped version of the photo was used for the cover of Philip Dray's lynching history *At the Hands of Persons Unknown* (2002). It is also the focus of a slim academic volume, *Lynching Photographs*, in the series Defining Moments in American Photography (Apel & Smith, 2007).
2. We allotted one forty-five-minute class period to the project each week—they sometimes became partial periods, in practice—plus several consecutive days during the last two weeks of the school year for revisions and final presentations. I attended class approximately four days a week, observing some of Munn's regular lessons, interviewing students about their progress, and sometimes providing feedback. This added presence, while it did not take time away from the full class, helped keep the project running smoothly, and allowed us to make efficient use of official "project days."

3. In this respect, I am following Toulmin, among others, who questions the pursuit of totalizing goals like certainty and absolute rationality and argues for a standard of reasonableness, in which arguments are made and evidence given, without aspiring to final description and with tolerance for a "variety of reasonable opinions." I have in mind, as well, works by C. Wright Mills (1959, pp. 129–131), Robert Bellah (1981), and, more recently, Michael Agger (2007), which argue for the impossibility of value-free social science and instead call for inquiry that engages values deliberately and responsibly.

Chapter 1 : "Life Is an Experiment"

1. Unless otherwise noted, the biographical information in this chapter comes from a series of interviews conducted with Bill Munn in April and May 2011.
2. Some of Munn's experiences working for the Kennedy campaign are documented in Boomhower, 2008, pp. 71–72.
3. This appears to reflect the influence of educational psychologist Sam Wineburg, who argues for the teaching of cognitive processes, such as corroboration between sources, that historians employ as they read (1991). Munn recalls having encountered Wineburg's work in professional publications of the period, although I cannot pinpoint a precise article. He would later teach a course in social studies methods at Ball State University using Wineburg's book, *Historical Thinking and Other Unnatural Acts* (2001). A highlighted copy sat on his classroom bookshelf when I visited in 2011, alongside other works of education and history.
4. The program officer for the Kellogg Foundation, John Beineke, was a former social studies teacher in the Marion Community Schools and an early supporter of the project. At that time, Beineke was nearing the end of a ten-year writing project, a generally laudatory biography of William Heard Kilpatrick, based in part on new access to Kilpatrick's diaries (1998). Beineke later served as dean of the College of Education at Arkansas State University and as a professor of education and, by courtesy, history.
5. This quotation is drawn from a grant proposal submitted by Bill Munn to the Kellogg Foundation, which is an unpublished document.
6. The photographs can be viewed online at http://wikimarion.org/Samuel_Plato.
7. The project is viewable at http://wikimarion.org/Glen_Eltzroth.

Chapter 2 : Learning-as-a-Service

1. This last point is drawn out more explicitly elsewhere—for example Dewey, 1899, p. 29.
2. This focus on immediate, small-scale communities is in keeping with the traditional "expanding environments" curriculum developed in these same years, under some Deweyan influence and with his general approval (Leriche, 1987). One would expect work to engage broader contexts and audiences as students mature.
3. I do not object to the idea that students would be proud of themselves and their learning or that they would want to show it to others. Some of the CHP students quoted in Chapter 4 of this book show this kind of motivation, and it does not strike me as inappropriate

when balanced with other values. My point is that the logic of Sizer's assessments stresses product-as-exhibition, sometimes at the expense of product-as-contribution.

4. Sizer poses a similar guiding question, placed in the mouth of his central character, Horace: "What's to Be Exhibited?" (Sizer, 1992, p. 104, capitalization in original). That said, backward planning as a curricular principle can be attributed not to Sizer or Wiggins but to Ralph Tyler (1949).
5. Within the Coalition, during the time of both Sizer and Wiggins, performances and exhibitions were roughly analogous, except that performances took place at the end of each course whereas exhibitions took place at the end of a student's high school career (Cushman, 1990).
6. I am inspired here by a passage from Dewey's late-career treatment of aesthetics, *Art as Experience* (1934, pp. 48–49). A treatise on the philosophy of art may seem an unlikely place to find insights on learning and assessment, but Dewey's conception of the subject matter is expansive enough to be applicable. He presents the aesthetic as a dimension of all human experience, and not primarily a matter of beauty, as one might expect, but of a certain heightened, whole quality of experience. Dewey is concerned to show that the making and the appreciating of artistic products are two similarly active, creative experiences. Both simultaneously involve experiencing and evaluating the product in its immediate qualities and anticipating or imagining the experience of the other party. The wholeness of either experience is associated with the ability to carry out both of these intertwined processes in a sensitive way.
7. The Foxfire phenomenon came to an abrupt halt in 1992 when its founder, Eliot Wigginton, confessed to charges of sexually abusing minors (Smothers, 1992). Wigginton was jailed and funding dried up. *Foxfire* continues to be published, albeit in a greatly reduced form (Gewertz, 2001). As a result of this scandal, *Foxfire* vanished from the American educational conversation and remains an uncomfortable subject to discuss. By no means do I intend to excuse or minimize Wigginton's crimes, but I feel obligated to include the program here as a way of acknowledging intellectual debt. *Foxfire* was one of several inspirations for Bill Munn's CHP, and I have found it to be an instructive example of learning that makes a difference.
8. The German social theorist Hans Joas, for example, has attempted to articulate how values arise through human action and experience—over the course of individual lives and, over a longer time scale, in a shared culture (1997, 2000, 2013). Though initially a scholar of G. H. Mead, Joas has been heavily influenced by Dewey, among others (Joas, 2000, chap. 7). Joas's account of value formation is friendly to religion and integrates insights from thinkers such as Charles Taylor. Although writing from a decidedly secularist perspective, philosopher Philip Kitcher has undertaken a similar project of reconstructing Deweyan ethics and explaining the development of ethical systems over the course of human history (2011).

Chapter 3 : History in the Act

1. Here, as throughout, students are referred to using pseudonyms. The privacy protection provided by these pseudonyms is limited, given that I make reference to publicly available products. The students and parents were made aware of this when granting consent, and

the students were given the option of publishing their work on WikiMarion anonymously, to provide heightened protection. I also gave students the option to read relevant portions of the book before its submission as a dissertation and, if desired, to remove their names from WikiMarion. None of these options was taken.

2. This and all interview protocols are provided in Appendix A.
3. The Munns paid for their own tickets, although Munn later received a $600 stipend for his participation that spring.
4. This question may have a basis in one concrete artifact. In 1921, under the direction of teacher Cora Straughan, a group of history students at Marion High School compiled a book titled *Lest We Forget: Reminiscences of the Pioneers of Grant County, Indiana*, which presents 140 pages of personal histories and lore (Straughan, 1921). As a project in 2007, a student annotated one of the entries, contextualizing it in terms of transportation, education, health, and other factors (http://wikimarion.org/William_and_Nancy_Maine). The project was successful and the idea remains ripe for further pedagogical experimentation.
5. Y was probably referring to page 9, on which Madison mentions a white accused murderer and black accused rapist who were playing cards in the jail when the mob entered. My notes are ambiguous, but this is the most reasonable interpretation.

Chapter 4 : "People Need to Know"

1. All student names are pseudonyms. For ease of reading, I have removed verbal tics and filler words such as "um," "like," "you know," and "kind of," except when they change the sense of the quotation. When quoting from students' published projects, I have retained occasional errors of spelling or grammar. I avoided marking these errors *sic* so as not to draw attention to them.
2. For example, his original questions were directed more toward lynching as a national phenomenon. I encouraged him to address issues of local and personal experience.
3. I had not yet turned on my voice recorder, so unlike most of the quotations in this chapter, it is taken from my written field notes and is therefore approximate.
4. This is evident later in this chapter, when Nick speaks of making a memorial.
5. Ashley, Michael, Lynn, and Julia said they did more research than usual. Jason, Alex, Alexis, and Carmen said they did a better job. Tom and Eric said they would advise students to be especially careful with work that will be posted on the Internet.
6. Nine of nineteen students voiced this concern.
7. One of my interview prompts included the word "interesting." In some, but not all interviews, I asked if students had shown their projects to anyone and, if so, what people were interested in. But in only one case did a student use the word in restating the question—and she had introduced the word previously without prompting. In nearly all instances, the word was used to describe Marion or the project or to compare the project with the first-semester paper.
8. This quotation is taken from my field notes of May 5, 2011, and may be approximate.

9. The formatting in this quotation is preserved from David's wiki page. The first two sentences were written by David whereas the question and answer are quotations from the Court of Inquiry transcript.
10. It seems to be rarer in interview projects, which more consistently yield powerful personal encounters and can, with an appropriate supporting written assignment, engage skills of contextualization, but which call on less in the way of critical analysis.
11. Thirteen of nineteen students mentioned talking to family members in this way.
12. Nine of nineteen students remarked on this increased sense that Marion was interesting or important.
13. Six of nineteen students spoke about how much Marion had changed since the time of the lynching.
14. As discussed by Novick (1988, p. 28), this common interpretation of Ranke may not be entirely appropriate. Ranke's German phrase, "*wie es eigentlich gewesen*." has often been translated into English as "as it really was" and has become associated with the hard-nosed empiricism of American historiography. Iggers (1973) argues that the phrase is better translated as "as it essentially was," which, interpreted in light of German idealism, signifies an interest more in capturing historical essences than in representing raw facts.

Chapter 5 : Realizing the Public Values of Learning

1. Martha Davis is a pseudonym, used at her request. All other interviewees in this chapter were given the option of being identified with a pseudonym but declined.
2. Ed Breen, Becky Boyle, and Rhonda Stoffer spoke positively about the multimedia and interactive aspects of the projects, as did three of the four historians. Tim Eckerle agreed that this was an important quality for a product to have but thought WikiMarion was not as "dynamic" as it might be.
3. As previously noted, Pattengale wrote a letter to the editor of the *Chronicle-Tribune* on the occasion of Munn's being named county historian, and he cites a CHP project as a historical source in his college-level textbook, *The Purpose-Guided Student* (2010).
4. Madison spoke about the pull of photographs for members of the public. Hawkins said that the use of "media, video, [and] pictures" would help to "sustain enthusiasm for the project." Pattengale praised the "full sensory engagement" of the website as a whole, gave "kudos" to Nick's map, and said it was "helpful" that it provided photographs of the buildings in addition to locations, "so that someone sitting in New Jersey could pull it up."
5. Warnock, for example, said certain projects were less "professionally done" than others, and faulted one project for referring to historical actors by their first names. Madison gave the writing a mixed assessment, calling out, among other things, a convoluted opening paragraph in which he "couldn't find a thesis statement." Both then moved on to other projects in which they found the writing to be more satisfactory. Pattengale noted a few minor proofreading errors, and Hawkins noticed an awkward phrasing that he regarded as typical of student writing.

6. See, for example, usability guru Jacob Nielsen's "How Users Read on the Web" (http://www.useit.com/alertbox/9710a.html). His answer begins, "They *don't*," with emphasis from the original.

Conclusion

1. Elmore cites not Sizer but Michael Sedlak and his colleagues' notion of a "bargain" between teachers and students: "You give me order and attendance, I'll give you passing grades and [minimal] homework" (Sedlak, Wheeler, Pullin, & Cusick, 1986).
2. The transcript is viewable at http://wikimarion.org/Elton_Vice.
3. The project Madison referenced did have lasting consequences. Built in 1928 to honor veterans of World War I, Memorial Coliseum was an important community center and the high school basketball arena until 1970. The project was completed skillfully by the sports-enthusiast son of the high school athletic director. At the time of the project, the coliseum sat derelict, but several years later, the local YMCA successfully petitioned the city council to buy and renovate the facility as its new home, citing the student's article in its presentation (Munn, personal interview, July 14, 2010).
4. Chapter 5 recounted the story of James Warnock's son, who interviewed his grandfather about opening Nazi concentration camps. I heard a similar story from Marion High School's long-time school nurse. Meeting her in the hallway on one of my first days back in town, I explained why I had returned, and she spontaneously told me how grateful she was to Mr. Munn. Her son, too, had interviewed a grandfather and elicited never-before-heard wartime stories. He had since passed away, and the recording had become a family treasure. Both Warnock's son and the nurse had done two CHP projects: one a report on the student's own house and one an interview with a grandfather. According to both parents, speaking independently, the interviews had greater lasting impact.
5. The website of the Oral History Association (http://oralhistory.org) publishes and collects numerous helpful resources, including a guide for students in grades four through twelve (Ardemendo & Kuszmar, n.d.).
6. A number of mobile applications have been developed along these lines. An early wave of applications dealt with individual regions, such as Cleveland Historical (http://clevelandhistorical.org), a project of Cleveland State University's Center for Public History & Digital Humanities. That project has since created a platform, Curatescape, for use by other regional projects. An alternative to the regional model, Marshall University's Clio app (http://theclio.com) serves as a single source for location-based historical entries nationwide. Clio has been used by university classes, with students creating content and faculty vetting it (Trowbridge, 2015).
7. Numerous top-level Common Core goals are addressed by CHP projects, including the following: "They use technology and digital media strategically and capably"; "They build strong content knowledge"; and, "They demonstrate independence." The expanded version of this last point says, "They become self-directed learners, effectively seeking out and using resources to assist them, including teachers, peers, and print and digital reference materials" (Common Core State Standards Initiative, 2010, p. 7).

REFERENCES

Adams, N. (2011, August 4). *Progress and promise for a town once in crisis*. Washington, DC: National Public Radio. Retrieved from http://www.npr.org/2011/08/04/138799351/progress-and-promise-for-a-town-once-in-crisis

Agger, M. (2007). *Public sociology: From social facts to literary acts*. Lanham, MD: Rowman & Littlefield.

Allen, J. (Ed.). (2000). *Without sanctuary: Lynching photography in America*. Santa Fe, NM: Twin Palms.

Apel, D., & Smith, S. M. (2007). *Lynching photographs*. Berkeley: University of California Press.

Ardemendo, D., & Kuszmar, K. (n.d.). *Principles and best practices for oral history education (4–12)*. Retrieved from http://www.oralhistory.org/wp-content/uploads/2014/04/2013-1411_Oral_History_ClassroomGuide_Update_V2.pdf

Bailey, T., Kennedy, D. M., & Cohen, L. (2001). *The American pageant: A history of the republic* (12th ed.). Boston, MA: Houghton Mifflin.

Ball, E. (1998). *Slaves in the family*. New York, NY: Farrar, Straus & Giroux.

Barab, S., & Duffy, T. (2000). From practice fields to communities of practice. In D. H. Jonanssen & S. M. Land (Eds.), *Theoretical foundations of learning environments* (Vol. 1, pp. 25–55). Mahwah, NJ: Lawrence Erlbaum.

Beineke, J. A. (1998). *And there were giants in the land: The life of William Heard Kilpatrick*. New York, NY: Peter Lang.

Bellah, R. (1981). The ethical aims of social inquiry. *Teachers College Record*, *83*(1), 1–18.

Bellah, R. N., Sullivan, W. M., Tipton, S. M., Swidler, A., & Madsen, R. P. (1985). *Habits of the heart: Individualism and commitment in modern life*. Berkeley: University of California Press.

Benkler, Y. (2006). *The wealth of networks: How social production transforms markets and freedom*. New Haven, CT: Yale University Press.

Blikstein, P. (2014). Digital fabrication and "making" in education: The democratization of invention. In J. Walter-Hermann & C. Buching (Eds.), *FabLabs: Of machines, makers and inventors* (pp. 203–222). Berlin, Germany: Verlag.

Booher, W. J. (2004, March 4). Church's growth leads it to Fishers. *The Indianapolis Star*, p. N1.

Boomhower, R. E. (2008). *Robert F. Kennedy and the 1968 Indiana primary*. Bloomington: Indiana University Press.

Brown, A. L., & Campione, J. C. (1994). Guided discovery in a community of learners. In K. McGilly (Ed.), *Classroom lessons: Integrating cognitive theory and classroom practices* (pp. 229–270). Cambridge, MA: MIT Press.

Cameron, J. (1994). *A time of terror: A survivor's story*. Baltimore, MD: Black Classic Press. (Original work published 1982)

Carr, C. (2006). *Our town: A heartland lynching, a haunted town, and the hidden history of white America*. New York, NY: Three Rivers Press.

Carr, E. H. (1967). *What is history?* London, England: Vintage.

Colley, A. J. (2008, July 6). Think you know Marion? *Chronicle-Tribune*.

Common Core State Standards Initiative. (2010). *Common Core State Standards for English language arts & literacy in history/social studies, science, and technical subjects*. Washington, DC: Author. Retrieved from http://www.corestandards.org/assets/CCSSI_ELA%20Standards.pdf

Crumrin, T., Bunch, L., & Munn, W. (2003). David Thelen's "Learning from the past": A conversation with the IMH. *Indiana Magazine of History*, 99(2), 165–171.

Cushman, K. (1990). Performance and exhibitions: The demonstration of mastery. *Horace*, 6(3), 1. Retrieved from http://archive.essentialschools.org/resources/123.html

Dewey, J. (1899). *The school and society*. Chicago: University of Chicago Press.

Dewey, J. (1902). *The child and the curriculum*. Chicago: University of Chicago Press.

Dewey, J. (1903). *Ethical principles underlying education*. Chicago: University of Chicago Press.

Dewey, J. (1927). *The public and its problems*. New York, NY: Holt.

Dewey, J. (1934). *Art as experience*. New York, NY: Perigee Books.

Dewey, J. (1939). Theory of valuation. In *International encyclopedia of unified science*. Chicago: University of Chicago Press.

Dewey, J., & Dewey, E. (2008). *Schools of to-morrow*. Mineola, NY: Dover.

Dillon, S. (2011, January 7). Journal showcases dying art of the research paper. *The New York Times*. Retrieved from http://www.nytimes.com/2011/01/08/education/08research.html

Dray, P. (2002). *At the hands of persons unknown: The lynching of black America*. New York, NY: Random House.

Elmore, R. (2011, May). What would happen if we let them go? *Education Week—the Futures of School Reform*. Retrieved from http://blogs.edweek.org/edweek/futures_of_reform/2011/05/what_would_happen_if_we_let_them_go.html

Eyler, J., & Giles, D. E., Jr. (1999). *Where's the learning in service-learning?* Indianapolis, IN: Jossey-Bass.

Frantz, D., & Collins, C. (2000). *Celebration, U.S.A.* New York, NY: Henry Holt.

Garrett, J. (Producer), Lehman, N. (Director). (1994). *A lynching in Marion* [Documentary]. United States: Wisconsin Public Television.

Gewertz, C. (2001, February 7). Financial difficulties force Foxfire to reduce outreach. *Education Week.*

Gottlieb, E., & Wineburg, S. (2012). Between *veritas* and *communitas*: Epistemic switching in the reading of academic and sacred history. *Journal of the Learning Sciences, 21*(1), 84–129.

Gouinlock, J. (1972). *John Dewey's philosophy of value*. New York, NY: Humanities Press.

Gould, T. (Producer). (1998). The Marion lynching of 1930 [Documentary]. In *Across Indiana*. United States: WFYI.

Habermas, J. (1989). *The structural transformation of the public sphere: An inquiry into a category of bourgeois society*. Cambridge, England: Polity.

Harty, K. (2003, October 14). Revote: No plaque. *Chronicle-Tribune.*

Hovde, E., & Meyer, M. (Directors). (1999). *American photography: A century of images* [Documentary]. United States: Middlemarch Films.

Iggers, G. (1973). Introduction. In Iggers, G. & Moltke, K. (Eds.) *The theory and practice of history*. Indianapolis, IN: Bobbs-Merrill.

Indy stage hosting play with Marion ties. (2011, April 8). *Chronicle-Tribune.*

James Cameron, 92, founder of museum, is dead. (2006, June 15). *The New York Times*. Retrieved from http://www.nytimes.com/2006/06/15/us/15cameron.html

Joas, H. (1997). *The creativity of action* (J. Gaines & P. Keast, Trans.). Chicago: University of Chicago Press.

Joas, H. (2000). *The genesis of values* (G. Moore, Trans.). Chicago: University of Chicago Press.

Joas, H. (2013). *The sacredness of the person: A new genealogy of human rights*. Washington, DC: Georgetown University Press.

Kilpatrick, W. H. (1918). *The project method: The use of the purposeful act in the educative process*. New York, NY: Teachers College, Columbia University.

Kitcher, P. (2011). *The ethical project*. Cambridge, MA: Harvard University Press.

Krajcik, J. S., & Blumenfeld, P. (2006). Project-based learning. In *The Cambridge handbook of the learning sciences* (pp. 317–334). Cambridge, England: Cambridge University Press.

Ladson-Billings, G. (1995). Toward a theory of culturally relevant pedagogy. *American Educational Research Journal, 32*(3), 465–491.

Leriche, L. W. (1987). The expanding environments sequence in elementary social studies: The origins. *Theory & Research in Social Education, 15*(3), 137–154.

Lynd, R., & Lynd, H. (1929). *Middletown: A study in modern American culture*. New York, NY: Harcourt.

Madison, J. H. (1986). *The Indiana way*. Bloomington: Indiana University Press.

Madison, J. H. (2001). *A lynching in the heartland: Race and memory in America*. New York, NY: Palgrave Macmillan.

Malcomson, S. (2001). *One drop of blood: The American misadventure of race*. New York, NY: Farrar, Straus and Giroux.

Manley, T., Jr., Buffa, A. S., Dube, C., & Reed, L. (2006). Putting the learning in service learning: From soup kitchen models to the black metropolis model. *Education and Urban Society*, *38*(2), 115–141.

Margolick, D. (2001). *Strange fruit: The biography of a song*. New York, NY: Harper Perennial.

Mills, C. W. (1959). *The sociological imagination*. New York, NY: Oxford University Press.

Munn, B. (n.d.). Final narrative report to the Kellogg Foundation: Community History Project.

Munn, B. (2000, January 5). Child labor was the subject of national, local news in 1911. *Chronicle-Tribune*, p. A4.

Munn, B., Bratton, S., & Lakes, T. (Eds.). (1999). *Rough times: Oral histories collected by students in Advanced Placement US History and Advanced Placement English at Marion High School, Marion Indiana, 1997–1998*. Marion, IN: Marion Public Library and Museum.

Novick, P. (1988). *That noble dream: The "objectivity question" and the American historical profession*. Cambridge, England: Cambridge University Press.

Papert, S. (1980). *Mindstorms: Children, computers, and powerful ideas*. New York, NY: Basic Books.

Papert, S. (1991). Situating constructionism. In S. Papert & I. Harel (Eds.), *Constructionism*. Norwood, NJ: Ablex.

Pattengale, J. (2008, June 17). Munn worthy of being named county historian. *Chronicle-Tribune*, p. A6.

Pattengale, J. (2010). *The purpose-guided student: Dream to succeed*. Boston, MA: McGraw-Hill Higher Education.

Patterson, O. (1998). *Rituals of blood: Consequences of slavery in two American centuries*. Washington, DC: Civitas Counterpoint.

Perdue, C. (1984). The Americanization of John Egerton and Auntie Arie. *Appalachian Journal*, *11*(4), 437–441.

Play chronicles Marion history. (2011, April 5). *Chronicle-Tribune*.

Preservation as progress [Editorial]. (1998, July 8). *Chronicle-Tribune*, p. A8.

Puckett, J. L. (1989). *Foxfire reconsidered: A twenty-year experiment in progressive education*. Urbana: University of Illinois Press.

Putnam, H. (2002). *The collapse of the fact/value dichotomy and other essays*. Cambridge, MA: Harvard University Press.

Ravitch, D. (2000). *Left back: A century of battles over school reform*. New York, NY: Simon & Schuster.

Robinson, L. (1998, February 19). Student documents local Underground Railroad. *Chronicle-Tribune*, p. A3.

Robinson, M. (2004). *Gilead*. New York, NY: Picador.

Sandel, M. (2011). Harvard University's Justice with Michael Sandel. Retrieved from http://www.justiceharvard.org/

Sapin, P. (Producer). (1995). *Unforgiven: Legacy of lynching* [Documentary]. United Kingdom: British Broadcasting Company.

Scardamalia, M. (2002). Collective cognitive responsibility for the advancement of knowledge. In B. Smith (Ed.), *Liberal education in a knowledge society* (pp. 67–98). Chicago, IL: Open Court.

Scardamalia, M., & Bereiter, C. (2006). Knowledge building: Theory, pedagogy, and technology. In R. K. Sawyer (Ed.), *The Cambridge handbook of the learning sciences* (pp. 97–115). Cambridge, England: Cambridge University Press.

School snapshot, Marion High School. (2011). Indiana Department of Education. Retrieved from http://mustang.doe.state.in.us/SEARCH/snapshot.cfm?schl=2351

Sedlak, M., Wheeler, C., Pullin, D., & Cusick, P. (1986). *Selling students short: Classroom bargains and academic reform in the American high school.* New York, NY: Teachers College Press.

Sharma, B. (2000, July 17). Teen-ager presents Indiana trucks: Marion High School students participate in Grant County Community History Project. *Chronicle-Tribune*, p. A4.

Shaw, B. (2000). Bias in bronze. *Indianapolis Star*, p. E2.

Show Choir Canada. (2010). The evolution of show choir. Toronto, ON, Canada: Author. Retrieved from http://www.showchoircanada.com/about-us/our-history

Sickler, A. P. (1998). *Miami Indians and the Mississinewa River*. WikiMarion. Retrieved from http://wikimarion.org/Miami_Indians_and_the_Mississinewa_River

Sigmon, R. (1979, Spring). Service-learning: Three principles. *Synergist,* 9–11.

Sizer, T. R. (1984). *Horace's compromise: The dilemma of the American high school.* Boston, MA: Houghton Mifflin.

Sizer, T. R. (1992). *Horace's school: Redesigning the American high school.* Boston, MA: Houghton Mifflin.

Sizer, T. R., & Sizer, N. F. (2000). *The students are watching: Schools and the moral contract.* Boston, MA: Beacon Press.

Smith, C. (Writer). (2011, April 1). *The Gospel according to James*. Live performance at the Indiana Theatre, Indianapolis, IN.

Smith, S. (1997, August 2). Generations join hands to collect vanishing history. *Chronicle-Tribune*, p. B4.

Smith, S. (1999, March 1). Students uncover area's forgotten past: Class projects end up on library website. *Chronicle-Tribune*, pp. A1, A2.

Smith, S. (2001, January 7). Marion teacher documents Underground Railroad sites. *Chronicle-Tribune*, p. D1.

Smith, S. (2002, January 1). David Blunk II is on a mission to find Samuel Plato structures: Marion senior turns his love of art, history into school project. *Chronicle-Tribune*, p. A5.

Smothers, R. (1992, November 13). "Foxfire book" teacher admits child molestation. *The New York Times*. Retrieved from http://www.nytimes.com/1992/11/13/us/foxfire-book-teacher-admits-child-molestation.html

Soep, E., & Chávez, V. (2010). *Drop that knowledge: Youth Radio stories*. Berkeley: University of California Press.

Stegner, W. (1987). *Crossing to safety*. New York, NY: Random House.

Straughan, C. (Ed.). (1921). *Lest we forget: Reminiscences of the pioneers of Grant County, Indiana*. Marion, IN: Printing Department of Marion High School.

Students for a Democratic Society. (1962). Port Huron statement. New York, NY: Author. Retrieved from http://www.h-net.org/~hst306/documents/huron.html

Thelen, D. (2003). Learning from the past: Individual experience and re-enactment. *Indiana Magazine of History*, 99(2), 155–165.

Town with tainted past elects first black sheriff in Indiana. (1998, November 7). *The Southeast Missourian*, p. 7A.

Trowbridge, D. (2015). Clio goes mobile: Connecting the public with the history that surrounds them [Web log post]. Retrieved from http://www.processhistory.org/?p=545

Tyler, R. W. (1949). *Basic principles of curriculum and instruction*. Chicago: University of Chicago Press.

U.S. Census Bureau. (1880). *Tenth census of the United States*. Washington, DC.

U.S. Census Bureau. (1900). *Twelfth census of the United States*. Washington, DC.

U.S. Census Bureau. (1970). *Nineteenth census of the United States*. Washington, DC.

U.S. Census Bureau. (2010). *Twenty-third census of the United States*. Washington, DC.

Vecchione, J. (Director). (1986). *Eyes on the prize: Awakening, 1954–1956* [Documentary]. United States: Blackside.

Voss, M. T. (1998). *Migration to freedom: The Underground Railroad in Grant County, Indiana*. WikiMarion. Retrieved from http://wikimarion.org/Migration_to_Freedom

Voss, M. T., & Sickler, A. P. (1999). *Weaver: Life at the crossroads*. WikiMarion. Retrieved from http://wikimarion.org/Life_at_the_Crossroads

Waters, A. (1999, June 24). Marion High School history project has its rewards. *Chronicle-Tribune*, p. A3.

Waters, A. (2000, January 9). Teacher, students produce book. *Chronicle-Tribune*, p. A3.

Waters, A. (2001a, January 19). Marion students surprised by history of county's buildings: Project connects students to area. *Chronicle-Tribune*, p. A3.

Waters, A. (2001b, July 20). History teacher, students receiving recognition. *Chronicle-Tribune*, p. A3.

Wiggins, G. (1989). Teaching to the (authentic) test. *Educational Leadership*, 46(7), 41–47.

Wiggins, G. (1993). Assessment: Authenticity, context, and validity. *Phi Delta Kappan*, *75*(3), 210–214.

Wiggins, G., & McTighe, J. (2005). *Understanding by design*. Alexandria, VA: Association for Supervision & Curriculum Development.

Wigginton, E. (Ed.). (1972). *The Foxfire book: Hog dressing, log cabin building, mountain crafts and foods, planting by the signs, snake lore, hunting tales, faith healing, moonshining, and other affairs of plain living*. Garden City, NY: Anchor Press/Doubleday.

Wineburg, S. (1991). Historical problem solving: A study of the cognitive processes used in the evaluation of documentary and pictorial evidence. *Journal of Educational Psychology*, 83(1), 73–87.

Wineburg, S. (2001). *Historical thinking and other unnatural acts: Charting the future of teaching the past*. Philadelphia, PA: Temple University Press.

Wright, W. (1999, April 3). History teacher given research fellowship. *Chronicle-Tribune*, p. A4.

INDEX

Studies in the Postmodern Theory of Education

General Editor
Shirley R. Steinberg

Counterpoints publishes the most compelling and imaginative books being written in education today. Grounded on the theoretical advances in criticalism, feminism, and postmodernism in the last two decades of the twentieth century, Counterpoints engages the meaning of these innovations in various forms of educational expression. Committed to the proposition that theoretical literature should be accessible to a variety of audiences, the series insists that its authors avoid esoteric and jargonistic languages that transform educational scholarship into an elite discourse for the initiated. Scholarly work matters only to the degree it affects consciousness and practice at multiple sites. Counterpoints' editorial policy is based on these principles and the ability of scholars to break new ground, to open new conversations, to go where educators have never gone before.

For additional information about this series or for the submission of manuscripts, please contact:

Shirley R. Steinberg
c/o Peter Lang Publishing, Inc.
29 Broadway, 18th floor
New York, New York 10006

To order other books in this series, please contact our Customer Service Department:

(800) 770-LANG (within the U.S.)
(212) 647-7706 (outside the U.S.)
(212) 647-7707 FAX

Or browse online by series:

www.peterlang.com